A Life of Dialogue

A Life of Dialogue

Love Letters to My Daughters

Kenneth Paul Kramer

RESOURCE *Publications* · Eugene, Oregon

A LIFE OF DIALOGUE
Love Letters to My Daughters

Copyright © 2016 Kenneth Paul Kramer. All rights reserved. Except for brief quotations in critical publications or reviews, no part of this book may be reproduced in any manner without prior written permission from the publisher. Write: Permissions, Wipf and Stock Publishers, 199 W. 8th Ave., Suite 3, Eugene, OR 97401.

Resource Publications
An Imprint of Wipf and Stock Publishers
199 W. 8th Ave., Suite 3
Eugene, OR 97401

www.wipfandstock.com

PAPERBACK ISBN: 978-1-4982-8955-9
HARDCOVER ISBN: 978-1-4982-8957-3
EBOOK ISBN: 978-1-4982-8956-6

Manufactured in the U.S.A.

You cannot lay bare your private soul and look at it. You are too much ashamed of yourself. For that reason . . . I'm not going to write autobiography. The man has yet to be born who could write the truth about himself.

—Mark Twain
Autobiography

To my Grandchildren.

Contents

Preface | xi

Stage I: Formative Years (1941–1963)

Earliest Memory | 3
The Bright-Eyed Boy | 6
No! | 8
Mom and Dad | 11
Walking with Roy | 14
Lipton Tea with Rose | 17
Alpha Baptist Church | 21
The Childhood Door | 23
Baptism | 25
Decision | 28
Sports, Sports, Sports | 31
Never Before | 33
Missed Free Throws | 35
On First Meeting Eliot and Buber | 39
Setting Forth | 42

Stage II: Leaving Home (1963–1974)

Andover Newton | 47
"The Travesty" | 51
Yale's Unexpected Calling | 54
First Class: First Day | 56
Finding Out | 59
"I'd Like to Get to Know You" | 62
Temple University Professors | 64

Phillips' "Let That Dilemma Be Your Way" | 66
DeMartino's "True Self is Awakening Awakening to Itself" | 69
Friedman's "All Real Living is Dialogic Encounter" | 71
Fidelity to the Task | 73
Baptist to Buddhist | 76
The Materializing Guru | 78
Loneliness | 82
The Forbidden Kiss | 86
The Gypsy Lady | 89
Leila Ann | 92

Stage III: Traveling West (1974–2000)

Santa Cruz | 97
Yvonne Rose | 102
SJSU | 105
"The Castilian Rose" | 108
"You No Longer Need to Sit" | 110
Holy Trinity Brothers | 113
October 11th | 117
Separation and Divorce | 121
In Each Other's Hearts | 124
Halfway Between University and Church | 126
From Crayons to Perfume | 128
The Faces of MS | 132
"I" Exam | 135
"Jesus, as a Jew, Would Never Have Said That" | 138
The Divine Comedian | 140
The Right Question for the Wrong Person | 142
Teaching on the Narrow Ridge | 144
The Limits of Dialogue | 148
"The Search Will Make You Free" | 150
What's Missing? | 152
Bowing Deeply | 155
Dialogic Awakening | 157
Dad's Death | 160
Mom's Death | 164
An Anonymous Student | 167

Stage IV: Retiring (2000– . . .)

Retirements | 173
Risking Enchantment | 175
A Large Cup of Java | 177
Sacramental Existence | 178
Still Swimming at Sixty-Five | 182
Twin Lakes Prayers | 184
Tuesdays with Todd | 186
Ever-Narrowing Confines | 191
The Turn Not Taken | 195
Weddings | 196
A Day in the Life at Seventy-Three | 199
Dark Moments | 202
The Rhythm of Sitting Here | 204
No More Needs to Be Said | 206
Trust with a Capital T | 209
My Brother | 211
"I Carry Your Heart" | 213
Cyberknifing | 216
Growing Up | 219
The Great Light | 222

Acknowledgments | 225
About the Author | 229

Preface

I sit alone at my second-hand, flea-market bought, extra-large, two-sided desk. Upon retiring, I taught myself to write with my left hand because my entire right side had become weakened by MS. A picture window opens out toward the pear tree at the center of the garden. Music fills the background: at times baroque, at times folk, at times monastic chanting, at times, silence. Fresh fruit and organic java with honey and a splash of half-and-half sit on the desk waiting their turn.

Time and space collaborate to make former stepping-stones present. Sitting in my electric wheel-chair, surrounded by hundreds of photocopied articles, journals, dreams, books and writings, I sip my coffee. I wait. Riding an unsuspected musical note, a word disembarks, and then another. I write because I cannot help myself.

Leila and Yvonne, you have undoubtedly been wondering what happened to the volume I had been working on for many years, the one you both asked me to write: "Since you've studied so many different religions and spiritual practices, what about your own journey? That's the one book of yours I'll read for sure." Now I share these autobiographical fragments as love letters to you both, taking you along with me on my life's journey.

MS provides me this extraordinary opportunity and time to focus even more on you, my daughters. I don't know when it first occurred to me that my body was carrying around a terrible mistake, a senseless irony, one that to this day contains no rational explanation. I won't go into great detail about all my symptoms and effects; it will however become obvious that my MS would rather have me discover what it – and it alone – makes possible in life than let it take away my soul. At times, MS speaks directly through me; at times, my voice is shaped by our dialogue.

Beyond that, telling my story seems a perfect legacy to leave you and my grandchildren. All of a sudden I look around and realize I'm it. I'm here at this flea-market-bought, extra-large, two-sided desk as the

Preface

elder of the family. I feel called to fulfill an age-old responsibility. Now 73, I have been convinced, perhaps mistakenly, that believing dialogically is a gift for mature years. As I approach the final mysterious gate, authentic interaction between us has become ever more auspicious. The archaic survivor speaks here of what is most hidden yet most redemptive, between himself and others.

I

Formative Years
(1941–1963)

Earliest Memory

Leila and Yvonne,

Long before memory had time to find me, there was only relationship. Nothing else existed. As far back as I can remember, it was a stranger's question that initiated my story. I was still in diapers in a playpen when, one afternoon, a visiting nurse stopped by to check on me. She looked over the side of the playpen as I was entertaining myself, grabbing this and pulling on that. A sweet smile brightened her face. The vivid sun illuminated the concrete as she and my mother talked.

"Mrs. Kramer," the nurse asked, "do you know what your son is going to be when he's grown?"

"No," my mother answered, surprised by the question. "I have no idea."

"I do." The nurse replied with certainty, a curiously playful look in her eye. "He's going to be a lawyer."

"Why do you say that?" my mother asked, puzzled yet intrigued.

"Watch him," she said, turning to look at me. "Look at how *curious* he is. He is interested in everything. He's going to make a good lawyer." Oblivious, I continued playing and banging.

Your grandmother was a woman of beauty, common sense, wisdom, and sweet, sweet grace who didn't want anything for herself. Beauty, because she never, ever wore make-up, except a little rouge on her cheeks. Wisdom? Not until you listened to her or, more often, she listened to you. And grace. This is the trickiest. To notice her grace, I think would require you to be around her for quite a while. No, for her whole life.

Once she caught me with my pants down in front of my cousin Nancy in her garage. Perhaps I was eight or nine.

"You show me yours, and I'll show you mine," I said, full of audacious confidence.

I — Formative Years (1941–1963)

When your grandmother showed up, the world halted. Her eyes were filled with shock, disappointment, and anger as she stood in the doorway, hand on her hip, strong, bold, and unmoving. Not only had it gone horribly wrong — that my mother, whom I idolized, had caught me — but I knew that when she told my father, he would hit me.

It was this man, after all, who once punched me in the jaw. I was six or seven at the time, but what happened remains remarkably vivid. I was sick and feverish so mom wanted my father to drive us to the doctor's office because she didn't drive. I remember him coming home in his brown United Parcel Service uniform, his short-sleeved shirt covering the American eagle tattoo on his left shoulder.

"Roy," my mother said as soon as he entered the living room, "Kenny's been sick. Can you take us to Doctor Bradford's?" She made small, graceful movements and spoke in a soft, unassuming tone.

Disgruntled, he shot back: "I'm hungry Rose. I want to eat first. Then I'll take him." He continued angrily banging around in the kitchen without missing a beat.

"But Kenny has a fever," she protested. She stood taller now, her voice stronger. I stood halfway between them. My father's back was to the front door and my mother's back was to the kitchen door.

"Goddammit Rose," he blasted. In one powerful motion, he sprang from the kitchen chair, shouting, "I'll take you after I eat!" His face flushed with blood-reddened anger, and he turned around, staring straight into her beautiful eyes. Usually, in my father's explosive moments, my mother retreated submissively.

Not this time. This time, she said, "Kenny, let's go! We'll walk," and she directed me toward the front door. I had never witnessed such defiance. Neither had my father. Instinctively, like a cornered bear, he swiped his huge paw-like hand at me. Just as I stepped toward the door, he struck me in the jaw with his fist with enough force to knock me onto the floor and across the room.

With unflappable determination, my mother reached out her hand to me: "Let's go!" That was all. Like a single strum on a guitar after the singer is finished, she said it again: "Let's go." My father didn't move, but we did. My sickness was completely forgotten. Off we walked, twenty minutes to the doctor's office near Broad and Allegheny Avenue. I was already feeling better.

Earliest Memory

But, what about Cousin Nancy, who didn't show me hers even though I showed her mine? What happened? First, mom talked to me about how what I did was wrong. I agreed. I knew it was wrong before I did it. That night, I cowered in my bedroom and waited for my father's inevitable footsteps to come up the stairs. When would she tell him?

Time passed with insane slowness, one second after the next. I kept expecting his footsteps. My heart was pounding. When would he come? I sat on the bed's edge, listening through the slightly cracked door, but I couldn't hear what they were talking about downstairs. "Kenny," my mother suddenly called up.

It was Zero hour!

"Time for cookies and milk before bed," she said.

What?

I went down very slowly, very softly. When I walked into the kitchen, my father was reading the evening paper, *The Philadelphia Bulletin*. Mom had placed several cookies on a white saucer next to a glass of milk.

No one spoke. I waited, but not a word was uttered. When I was finished, I got up slowly, softly, and walked upstairs. Nothing was said. Nothing was ever said. Gradually, in a few days, I stopped waiting. She never told him. And she never told me why she never told him.

As you know, my relationship with your grandmother has always been immensely vital to me, so much so that mystory must begin with my mother. No, not just with her, but with the dynamic interactions between the three of us. From beginning to end, my life unfolds as a testimony to my ongoing relationship with your grandmother Rose, one that comforts me, and with your grandfather Roy, one that challenges me.

The Bright-Eyed Boy

My Beautiful Daughters,

Oh, the freedom, the uncontested joy when I re-experience those wildly carefree moments, when the unknown landslide of play has its way with me. Early on, I wanted to become one of those respected enough to be chosen first for the good team first. This was long before I felt sympathy for the one chosen last. Picture a clean-cut kid with bright blue eyes, crew cut, patched jeans, a polo shirt, and sneakers, just wanting to play with the best.

I didn't want to ride wild horses with flowing manes — in fact, I was allergic to horses — nor did I want to chase the great wind down the mountain. I wanted to play with other kids in the same spirit, though, of abandoning everything for the play itself. I wanted to exceed. An only child, I wanted to become one of those in the front, and my heart was racing like a dream.

I did not want to become like my father: a hunter, a truck driver, and a gun collector. I remember one evening, when I was about ten, sitting on Aunt Leah's Quakertown porch after supper.

"Get rid of it, Roy," Aunt Leah yelled, fearing that a black kitten who had wandered onto the property would dig up her garden. Jumping through the grass, the small, soft kitten looked cuddly to me.

Without saying a word, my dad got up and walked into the house. I thought he would return with a broom to scare the kitty away. Instead, he returned with a silver pistol and quietly descended the porch stairs. I was scared, and stuck to my seat. I didn't dare speak.

"Here kitty, here kitty," he said.

As the kitten slowly moved toward him, perhaps expecting a treat, I saw father lift his arm and point the gun. In one moment, the kitten paused to sniff the grass. In the next moment my father squeezed the trigger. In one moment, the sun was reflected against motionless black fur lying on the green grass. In the next moment, dad planted black furred death in a shallow grave.

Why? . . . Why?

I hope I have never excessively scared you or even acted that cold and callous with you girls. I have passed on some of my father's redeeming qualities to you, along with, unfortunately, his self-centered, demanding nature.

No. I wanted to be like my mother who, without naming it, taught me the joy, the value, the recuperative power of genuine dialogue. She spoke in her unassuming way with remarkable ordinariness, yet with unmistakable love. Her eyes smiled through her perpetually tired face, a face marked by years of overtime service and hard work.

I wanted to be like her. What I didn't (couldn't) know was how impossibly difficult that would be.

No!

Sweethearts,

Do you remember when I took you to Philadelphia and showed you the brown brick, two-story row house with a full basement at 652 West Clearfield Street where I grew up? It was a short walk to the East-West trolley track at Allegheny Avenue and to the North-South track on 6th Street. Before signing the final real estate papers when my parents sold the house for four thousand dollars to buy one on an acre in Lower Trumbaursville near Quakertown, PA for twenty-five thousand, giving up the trolleys caused my mother to cry. She didn't drive. She knew she'd be trapped in a country house, completely dependent on my father.

    The front door of the Clearfield Street house opened into an entryway where, in the winter, we left our galoshes, coats, hats, gloves, and scarves when we came in from the snowy, blistering cold. But the house was kept toasty by the coal-burning furnace in the basement. I remember playing in the coal bin as a kid. Fortunately, there was a large concrete laundry basin nearby, where my mother gave me many baths after I came home filthy from playing in the streets. I loved each bath in that basin where she cleaned and wrung our dry laundry, cranking it through the rubber rollers with a handle.

    The entry door opened out into the rectangular, ugly-wallpapered living room, then through a door to the Formica-beige kitchen table and the ice-box, then through another door to a much smaller, shed-like room, which only had a stove, a sink, and a counter, where mother prepared food, and then to the back door, which led outside to a small concrete yard separated from the adjacent concrete yards of the attached houses to each side. That was it. In the summer, I would leave my two-wheeler in the yard; in the winter, my sled. Standing in the tiny backyard, one house from the corner, I could watch people and cars passing on 7th Street. But more often than not, I was outside.

One grey morning, I had raced up the stairs to avoid being confronted by my mom. I had done, mis-done, or not done something for which an accounting was due. Looking up from the bottom of the stairs, she saw her ten-year-old son in crew cut blue jeans, black high-top converse sneakers, and a blue polo shirt, looking down to see if she was going to run up.

She was very, very upset.

It might have been because I hadn't taken my lunch dishes to the sink, or because I left some games scattered in the living room, or because I didn't fully close the front door when I raced back outside after finishing lunch, or ... I don't remember. I just remember that she was very, very upset as she looked up at me from the bottom of the stairs.

"Kenneth!" she called up. When things were fine between us, she called me "Kenny." "Kenneth, come down here!" she yelled, her hand on her hip, pointing down toward the rug at the bottom of the stairs.

In the split second that followed, I did something I had never done before. For that matter, something I never did again. Even though it felt like I was denying the very existence of God, I yelled back with a furrowed brow, "NO!"

Silence.

I was shocked. Mother, I'm sure (well, maybe not) was shocked. Now what?! Would she run upstairs and punish me? No. Not that. What she did instead, as she was able to do in other extremely difficult moments, modeled for me how I would later become a parent.

Looking up at me, as if she knew something that I didn't, as if she trusted somewhere that I couldn't, with "amazing grace," she softly shifted her position, and in a calm tone answered, "Then go to your room. Don't leave it until you're ready to come down and talk."

Looking back, it's easy to realize how effective her response was. Not that she knew it consciously, of course, but her words gave me time to calm down, to rethink what I had just done, to feel the depths of my guilt, and, most importantly, to worry about what Dad would do. I sat on the bed with these different perspectives angling through my head before I went down, and we talked, and it became easy again, before going back outside to play.

I'm sure you remember, girls, the time we lived in a condo in Santa Cruz and I asked you each to clean up your room. When I discovered that it hadn't been done (that, in fact, it was worse than the last time I had seen

I—Formative Years (1941–1963)

it), I immediately threw all of your clothes and toys and games into a big pile in the center of the room.

And then I'm sure you remember what happened next: I picked each of you up by your arms and tossed you into that pile of clothes and screamed, "Don't come out until it's clean!" How I wish I could have acted as gracefully in your moments of defiance as your grandmother had done with me. I'm afraid, however, that my father's anger often overrode her grace.

Mom and Dad

Dearest Yvonne and Leila,

No matter how much I accept it (in relation to my mother) or resist it (in relation to my father), I am a continuation of my parents, Rose and Roy. Hopefully, with less anxiousness than Mom (ha!) and less anger/frustration than Dad (really?).

Hopefully, too, with Mom's sense of loving service and dad's fidelity to the task. I know that she — untrained and unread — introduced me to empathic dialogue, and I hope I have taken it to the next step. And I know that he introduced me to collecting books, and I hope I have refined the practice.

Aside from their similar backgrounds (she a German-Irish Protestant, and he a German Protestant), educations (in order to help support their families, neither finished high school), social niche (lower middle class, with mom from Baltimore, and dad from North Philly), almost everything else about them was different.

My mother was a survivor. "Rose do this, Rose do that," came endlessly from my father's mouth. I can still hear his demands. Talk about "old school." In my father's world, the male sat at the top of the authority pyramid in the home. Women sat at the bottom, holding the family together (although he would have said that he was responsible for doing that as well).

My decision not to enter the Ministry disappointed him greatly. He never understood why or how I could choose teaching over preaching, or liberating minds over saving souls — as if one's soul could ever be once-and-for-all saved. For him, given the world in which he was raised, a Baptist pastor possessed greater status than a university professor.

I wish I had asked each of them about their early relationship, especially since only one letter survives that ever-so-slightly pulls back the curtain. I still remember how surprised I was when, looking through a box of

I—Formative Years (1941–1963)

old pictures, I discovered the three-page handwritten letter (dated June 28, 1938) from my father to his future wife. It begins by referring to my dad's feelings of loneliness — a depth of which I never knew he felt.

> Dear Honey:
>
> Here it is Tuesday night and I feel as I am all alone in the world. We arrived home safely but the weather was bad. We ran into the storm at Curryville. It rained hard for a while then stopped. Then it was a fine rain until we were passing through Chester, then it rained so hard you had a hard time seeing the road. The wires on the bus got wet and the motor stopped. Luckily I was under a bridge. I dried the wires out (fifteen minutes lost) and didn't have any more trouble. It seems ages since I saw you last. Honey, I sure do miss you. You are on my mind continuously.

In the carefully scripted letter to his "Honey" who was in Baltimore at the time, he spoke of the difficulty he had driving his mother through a thunderstorm:

> We arrived home safely but the weather was bad. We ran into the storm at Curryville. It rained hard for a while then stopped. Then it was a fine rain until we were passing through Chester, then it rained so hard you had a hard time seeing the road. The wires on the bus got wet and the motor stopped. Luckily I was under a bridge. I dried the wires out (fifteen minutes lost) and didn't have any more trouble.

I most admired my father's ability to handle adversity, his ability to fix things, and his ability to make things:

> Honey, I believe I will not get a bathing suit this week, as I would like to have money over the weekend, that is to have enough as you never know when you need more. Let me know what you think of this?

Your grandfather's frugality is also clearly evident here.

His frugality, which my mother shared, meant that while we never had any extra, we always had enough. I remember always having hot dogs and beans on Friday night until my mother had money to shop on Saturday. I learned an extremely valuable lesson from my parents in this regard, one that guides me to this day. You girls know — I did my best to pass it on to you. We always had just enough, which is also probably why you always thought I should spend more money on you!

He finished the letter with an intense flourish of loving energy, that, unfortunately, I never received from him in my life:

> Honey, this is all I can think of now outside of you. I can't wait 'til Saturday when we will be together again. Give my love to mother and dad. (Tell mother to take good care of my girl Rosie.)
>
> Goodbye Honey 'til Saturday.
>
> Tons of Love,
>
> Your boy Gus

It brings me joy and deep satisfaction to know that, at the beginning of their relationship at least, my mother received this ever-so-brief, elated positive attention from my father (who was called Gus by his close friends). Soon, it would fade; then it would die. I never saw any of it. The dementia that she experienced in her later life was undoubtedly spurred by years of his emotional and psychological abuse.

As I reread these last lines, I recalled that once, buoyed by the eye-opening tradition-busting spirit of my undergraduate classes, I said to her, "Why don't you divorce dad? Your life would be so much better without him." I was convinced that she knew the truth of what I was saying, which is why her reply startled me.

"I can't leave your father, Kenneth. He needs me."

How could she say/believe/live that?

How?

I wouldn't begin to understand it until years later.

Walking with Roy

My Determined Daughters,

Here's a little more about my father because none of us really got to know him. Did he get to know himself, I've always wondered.

When I first heard the word "indefatigable," I was too young to recognize that my father was the walking image of its definition.

My father was a 6' 3", muscular, and handsome. He had Germanic features and straight, light brown hair, always neatly combed. He was a fighter who usually resisted any attempts to convince him that he was wrong about anything. Beneath the surface, he waged a struggle on some distant battlefield, in a location unknown to me. He was usually on the point of losing his temper, whether with my mother or with me, or with whomever he just saw, or with whatever he was doing. I grew up trying to keep my distance.

The big question was whether my father ever took a look at himself. I had no way of knowing whether he had felt guilty about handing on his increasingly cantankerous language — everything was "son of a bitch!" or "God damn it!" or "Jesus Christ!" — or his hostile demeanor, or his disrespectful interactions with the family.

My dad was raised by an angry but talented father and a meek mother who never said much. In my father's early years, his dad Paul was bedridden, with an unknown disease (likely MS). It was because of my grandfather's physical deterioration that Roy never finished junior high school, instead helping his mother, Mary. I can only imagine how much frustration and anger he must have picked up along the way.

What saved me was that I was able to gain intellectual freedom from him early on. But I didn't gain it fully until I published my first book, *World Scriptures*, which I dedicated to my parents, "Who know me better than any person alive and love me anyway!"

From the moment I decided to attend graduate school, I was able to begin building a bridge over and away from his influence. There were undoubtedly things we kept quiet about in each other's presence: my father had questions he harbored about religion; I had questions I harbored about girls and sexuality. As a result, I was left to leaf through girly magazines and have back alley conversations to inform my innocent ignorance, and I never learned how to lie.

After the playwright Samuel Beckett's father died, he remarked that he would never again know anyone like him. Although, I can't write about him, Beckett noted: I can only walk the fields and climb the ditches after him. Beckett's words deeply move me. In death, he honored his father's life by walking and climbing the exact places his father had walked and climbed. I, too, think of my father in this way, with powerful memories (though far too few) of walking with him.

I remember one Thanksgiving primarily because Dad took me to the annual high school football game between Northeast High, where Mom worked in the teacher's cafeteria, and Central High, where I was in my freshman year. I remember nothing of the game except that I marveled at how Central's quarterback avoided pressure from Northeast's hard charging linemen and completed several beautiful spirals. The total excitement captivated me.

It was the exhilaration of our half hour walk to the game that bonded me to my father, though, and not the game itself. My father was a man of few words, so whatever talking that transpired between us was mostly informational and perfunctory.

How unlike this was from the Sundays, walking for a half hour to Church with my mother, who filled the air with intriguing conversation. As a teenager, though, walking with my father gave me a reason to be proud of him.

A muscular six foot three inches, and a solid one hundred and ninety pounds, he could walk all day long. He took long strides, looking straight ahead, always ready to react to anything that might interrupt our progress.

I don't remember what we talked about on these walks. He never had much to say, and I was always too afraid of him to say much myself. It was still only partially obvious to me that we lived in two different worlds. Not finishing junior high school in order to support his mother, when his father died, he drove a Heinz 57 Varieties delivery truck and then a Wanamaker Furniture delivery truck.

I—Formative Years (1941–1963)

He was an outdoorsman, hunter, and collector of guns, rifles, and bullets, each of which he carefully arranged in his basement workshop. Never interested in guns myself, after he died I sold them all through a gun dealer.

For the most part, he kept me out of his world. Sure, he once gave me a .22 rifle as a Christmas present, but he immediately took it back for safekeeping. I never saw it again. I inhabited, instead, the world of teenage sports: stick ball, half ball, box ball, wire ball, football, and hose ball. I also played organized sports like recreation league basketball, church league bowling, and recreational league baseball.

But now, we walked as one: stepping, breathing, and heading toward the game. Walking in concert with his powerful strides—him setting the pace, me complementing it—I was completely happy.

Lipton Tea with Rose

My Compassionate Daughters,

As you girls remember, even aged and wrinkled, your grandmother was beautiful. But when she was young, she was soft. Her wavy dark chestnut hair set off her hazel eyes through which shone happiness, even if she was surrounded by unpleasantness. She never painted her nails, never smoked cigarettes, and never had a sip of alcohol in her entire life. She always said, "An alcoholic never knows he's an alcoholic before taking the first drink."

Indeed. My mother's father, Thomas Tracey, was a mechanical draftsman, and he drank his salary away every Friday night after receiving his paycheck. My mother's mother, Rose Leonhardt, was the major influence on my mother. It was from her that my mother learned unconditional love. "What's important are a person's deeds, not their words. Words without deeds are useless," she always said.

Every Easter, she would make sure that I had enough money to buy myself an Easter outfit. When I asked her about hers, she would always say, "Oh, I like the one that I wore last Easter." Only later did I discover that she only had enough money for me. She was a powerfully understated woman, yet here's what I most remember about her.

During my high school and college days, we would often sit and talk, each with a cup of black Lipton tea, around the shiny, yellowish-tan Formica kitchen table. It was my mother who opened the most important door of my life: the doorway to genuine dialogue. My favorite times were talking to her: while walking or drying the dishes, on the trolley car, or (my favorite) sitting around that ugly kitchen table with our cup of tea. We talked mostly about my life, my fun, my difficulties, my hopes, and my thoughts. She was the only person interested in what I was thinking and why.

"That's one of the reasons I used to love coming to your house," an old friend from Philly, Charles Longbottom told me. It surprised me to hear

I—Formative Years (1941–1963)

him say, "Your mom was always telling you of her love for you in different ways. That's why you grew up with such trust. You never thought about not succeeding, did you?"

We would talk about my classes, my friends, and the girls I dated. Often, several of my friends would visit me just to join in and I later learned that she would invite my childhood friend, Buddy Dykes, to eat Saturday morning breakfasts with me just so that I would begin to get used to sharing with others, and that she'd let me fight Ronnie Heintz in front of the house rolling in the milk wagon's horse manure because he had continued to bully her son. She would also explain why she would never divorce her husband (as I had once asked her to do) despite his psychological abuse: she had taken a vow in the sight of God never to do that. While I didn't agree, I listened carefully.

We chatted more about girls, about school, about a book she was reading, *The Power of Positive Thinking*, about dad, about why she stayed with him, about Alpha Church activities, about her work at the Northeast High School teacher's dining room, and even more about girls. Through all of it, as we drank our tea with milk and honey, there were three voices speaking—hers, mine, and as I would later learn, the voice of interaction itself.

And what did she say?

"The mind is like a garden, it needs to be cultivated."

"If you are feeling low and depressed, find someone who needs you more than you need them, and do something for them."

"I could never leave your father: it wouldn't be right."

"You know that my favorite singer is Mario Lanza."

"Your Uncle Bob lost all the money that he gave to his son-in-law to help him start a new business."

"Actions speak louder than words."

Surely you girls must remember lots of things that I have said to you over the years, many of which were influenced by my mother's sayings.

The clock never seemed to matter. Time was never present. Longbottom and Kashow liked coming to my house so that they could join in the dialogue with her. It was a good time, with some advice, some tea, some laughter, and hallowing relationships.

I would often tell you that my relationship with Rose did not end when she died, that it can never end in this life, and that all I have to do is to ask her what she thinks or feels about something, and her response is present to me in the third voice.

"Always open the door for a girl; let her go first; reach back to offer your hand when you disembark; always walk between her and the street."

"Why?" I once asked.

"To protect her from getting splashed if a car drives through a puddle as you walk by."

More important than what she said, but within it, and behind it, it was obvious that she felt deep empathy for other people.

Whenever I tell someone about her, I always recall how she would willingly seek out and listen to those whom no one else wanted to help. This willingness shaped me, shaped my relationship with life, with family, with nature, and with this moment's God.

Of course, if Rose ever heard me talk like this, in her usual self-effacing tone she would say, "Kenneth! I only did what any mother would do."

I remember standing off to the side of the choir after morning church service, watching and waiting and hungry and impatient with her. Everyone had left. She was listening to Francis rattle on about her uncertainties and fears and anxieties and doubts. On the way home, when I asked her, "Why do you remain week after week to talk with this forty-year old spinster woman who is still living with her mother and still doing what her mother wants her to do (like coming to church, and not getting married)?" Mom said, "Because no one else will listen to her."

I knew full well that when she warned me to "be careful not to act like your father does" that she was referring to actions far more belittling and nightmarish than she ever would mention. I still remember her second visit to Santa Cruz, this time to see our new house. I was standing with her at the sliding glass door in the family room and looking out into the large garden where my father was investigating the new territory.

"There are many things I have learned from you, and continue to learn from you," I said, "but can you tell me what in the world I have learned from him?" I said, looking first at my mom and then at my father inspecting the property line. Who knows what he was looking at or looking for; it just felt wonderful that he had the opportunity to see the large backyard that I had been able to buy, one like the acre of land that stretched out from his house near Quakertown.

After pausing for a moment or two she said, "You never leave anything you start unfinished. You learned that from him."

Years later, after my parents moved to California and were being cared for in a nursing home, my dear friend Mechthild would make a weekly

I—Formative Years (1941–1963)

visit to Rose. One day, when it was time to leave, Mechthild said, "Rose, I'm going to see your son."

And, through her dementia, my mother replied, "He blesses me."

Alpha Baptist Church

Yvonne and Leila,

The Alpha Baptist Church at Hancock and York Streets in Kensington, Philadelphia was the center of my religious life both before my baptism and until I left home at age twenty-one. For years on Sundays, I attended four services: "Church" from 10:30-12 a.m.; Sunday school from 1:30-2:30 p.m.; Baptist Youth Fellowship (B.Y.F.) from 6:30-7:45 p.m.; and evening Church from 8-9 p.m.

My mother hoped that Pastor Howard K. Williams — the silver-haired minister who was the sole shepherd of his flock for fifty-seven years before retiring — would become a spiritual father for me. This never quite happened, but he did form my image of an idealistic pastor.

During the summer months, the evening service was held on the church roof and was accompanied by a peculiar fruit-like scent that I have never smelled since, and that I still lack the words to adequately to describe. A fresh, honey-mint-aroma perfumed the choir's singing of hymns, many of which Pastor Williams had written for his flock.

As an undergrad student at Temple University, I began taking notes on his homilies, including seven sets of a Good Friday sermon, one on each of Jesus' last words. Between noon and 3 pm in that church, I was learning how sermons are constructed.

As a teenager, I swallowed Baptist beliefs and practices literally and wholly. On a Green Lake retreat, however, I experienced peak moments both alone in nature and with other young Baptists from around the country, and was first introduced to the idea of "symbolic meaning," a phrase used by William Hamilton of Colgate Rochester Divinity School. He said, "Jesus' teaching can be understood as pointing to something more than is contained in a literal interpretation."

WHAT? Where had I been?

I—Formative Years (1941–1963)

Yet it was the Church building itself that left the deepest impression on me. To the left of the pulpit in Alpha Baptist Church (from the congregation's point of view) was a large wooden organ with silver pipes that were played for years by Robert Plimpton. Robert Plimpton. I can't forget him. We became friends, and I drove out to Eastern Baptist College's campus where he was a student and where he had access to a large console organ, "God's instrument," as he called it.

Seated on the bench beside him, I watched as he vigorously depressed keys on the various keyboards, pulled out ivory stops on the side of the console to make pipe sounds, and quickly moved his feet over the wood pedals. I was forever impressed when he told me that he practiced playing the organ for five hours a day. Little did I know then that, later in my life, I would come to practice writing for five hours a day.

To the right of the pulpit was a small, rectangular raised tile pool (only large enough to accommodate two people) where, once a year, full immersion baptisms occurred. Over the pool, hung a large replica of Jesus praying at Gethsemane. Often, especially when I was younger and day-dreaming my way through a sermon, I would gaze up at the haloed picture of Jesus praying on his knees.

What was he praying for? For his Father's mercy and guidance, no doubt. The Lord's Prayer, no doubt. The art of praying—talking to the creator of everything and all, no doubt. The unfinished gift that Alpha gave me, that Pastor Williams and the congregation gave me, and that Jesus gave me was the inestimable value of prayer.

The main reason I'm including this otherwise seemingly boring letter to you girls is because here is where the significance of prayer was implanted into my life. And I mean utter significance, for while all religious forms will eventually fall away for me, prayer will not. The power of prayer, by which I mean something much different than the prayers of my youth, remains, so much so, that contemplative prayer is the unwritten foreword of all my writing.

Living a life of prayer for me started way back then. However, I always felt that prayer was a duty as well. It never seemed to generate instant happiness, other than knowing it would please my mother.

When you are around the same age as I was here, Leila and Yvonne, I hope you'll understand why I was so eager for you to attend church with me.

The Childhood Door

Playful Ones,

The novelist Graham Greene once wrote that there is always a moment in childhood when the door opens and lets the future in. For me, this was a moment in my childhood—a single event. It would have passed like other eventless moments, except what made it special was my innocence.

In the summer of my twelfth year, I was visiting my aunt and uncle in Quakertown. I always looked forward to these annual, weeklong summer visits to the country. Growing up on a street with no trees, their five acres of open green expanded my city-limited horizons.

After lunch, I saw a bullfrog sitting at the pond's edge. Slowly, I snuck up on it and stood quietly over it so as not to scare it. Blood was coursing through my veins. I grabbed my kid-sized, metal-tipped wooden arrow. The excitement of the kill drew the string back; I let it fly. Right through the frog's back. So *this* was the excitement dad felt when hunting wild animals. As I watched the frog, now pinned to the muddy ground, I saw it struggling to breathe. I had thought that this death would be immediate, but it took a while longer for it to finally stop breathing. Almost as if I was afraid of it, I ran off.

In the lazy early evening, I lost myself lying on the cool green lawn beneath the quiet grape arbor. I dissolved into a trance. Crickets, frogs, and birds performed early evening choral music, accentuating the wonderful smell of freshly mown grass. I loved that smell.

Lying flat on my back, looking up at the cloudless sky, I began considering questions that were brand new to me. I wondered, as I looked up, what existed on the other side of the sky? Is there more sky? And what's beyond that? What would happen if you could keep going higher and higher? Does the world have an end? For some reason, that possibility seemed impossible to me in that twilight moment.

I — Formative Years (1941–1963)

Stretching my head back to take in as much sky as I could, I continued to wonder: can you just keep going? How far away is it? Does anyone know? I was, for the first time, completely enveloped in mystery. I didn't know the answers to my questions, but I suspected that it was extremely important to know them and that I never actually would.

I was suddenly and gently seized by a question more profound than my young spirit could bear, and began to recognize the presence of inward awe. I felt compelled to listen to the silence, but I was too young to know how to weep for awe's sake, which, I would later discover, is described at the end of T.S. Eliot's youthful (1910) poem, "Silence."

> At such peace I am terrified.
> There is nothing else beside.

This, Eliot wrote, "is the ultimate hour/When life is justified."

Alas, the moment didn't last long. Molly, my aunt and uncle's dog who had been out chasing varmints, returned for a drink of water, I started thinking about my two favorite Philadelphia Phillies players, and then I was thirsty, and then as quickly as it descended upon me, the wonderment of that moment left.

Perhaps that experience was an early encounter with the mystery that my mother called God. However, rudimentary it was, I sensed that I could never know that mystery.

Did you ever have an experience in which you keep getting taken higher and, at the same, time kept getting taken deeper?

I've noticed as I've moved through life that such transformational moments have yielded often unanswerable questions just at the right time, and it's always seemed to me that these have come at just the right time.

When I discussed this event with my mother later, asking why I couldn't hold on to it, she leaned back in her chair and said, "No one can, Kenneth. It's part of the mystery of God's creation." Still to this day, girls, I remain guided by that real, but unknowable mystery. Pursuit of infinite mystery would become the driving force behind my later studies, teaching, and writing.

Baptism

My Precious Daughters,

What separates Baptists from other Protestants—from all other Christians, for that matter—is the rite of adult baptism, in which the believer is fully immersed in a pool of water as Jesus was fully immersed in the river Jordan by John the Baptizer. Its symbolism is powerful: the death of the old, sinful person and the birth of the new, righteous person.

This was more than I, as a thirteen year old, could grasp. Yet I knew from watching others over the years that baptism was the main deal. Everything in the Baptist faith led up to its centrality in a person's life. This ritual was the first real test of my faith, the first demonstration of my surrender to God's will.

The only sound made by any of the thirteen-year-olds in the church's baptismal dressing room was an occasional nervous cough or excited snickering. I remember wondering why no one spoke as we put on our long, black, rubberized baptismal robes, which were weighted with extra fabric at the bottom. My bell-shaped, pleated robe fit snugly, permitting only the top of my wide Windsor knot and the top half of my white collar to be seen.

I had never been in the hallway behind the pool before. It felt like I was walking inside a mystery. Each time the door separating the pool and congregation from the pre-baptized opened, I was given a partial view of the swollen Easter congregation in the auditorium.

Turning to the boy behind me, I whispered, "Are you scared?"

"Sure I am," he said. "Aren't you?"

"No, of course not," I whispered, but though I had eaten a double breakfast that morning, my stomach felt weak and undernourished. I watched the brown door open. The first boy returned noiselessly, leaving the carpet wet. I wanted to speak to him, but didn't.

I—Formative Years (1941–1963)

A quiet fear rang loudly in my ears. The hallway was free from activity. An unknown serenity settled on the already tranquil children, like fog blanketing a city. My eyes followed the line where the rug ended and the wall began. They came to rest on a spot where the water was peacefully held in a depression in the rug. I thought of the poor janitor who would have to mop up. It would be fine with me to be the janitor. I wouldn't mind cleaning up. Besides, it would be fun to swing the big mop.

The pool door opened wider this time. The quiet rushed in and wove itself into the hallway's silence. I looked past the pool into the large auditorium and saw men and women eager, but restrained, leaning forward to gaze over the balcony. Everyone was smiling.

The door gently swung back to its place in the open wall. The second boy returned from the pool and winked at me as if to say, "Don't be afraid."

"I'm not afraid!" I almost blurted, but the mystery of the hallway seduced me.

Silent steam slowly danced from the radiators on the wall. The hallway grew humid and beads of sweat formed on my forehead, rolling down one side of my nose and finding a path to my half-parted lips.

The unfathomable silence became deeper and more sonorous. It penetrated me. I wanted to speak. I wanted to shout. Anything. I raised my head, but I didn't see the pool door open. I didn't see the quiet water gently moving.

As an explosion dulls then sharpens the senses, I was shocked into a tumult when two hands pushed hard on my shoulders, snapping back my head as I stepped forward. I was next.

I stood motionless at the top of the pool steps. Howard K. beckoned. My legs locked. My face reddened.

"Ken, Ken," whispered Pastor Williams urgently. "Ken, come on what are you waiting for?"

I couldn't answer. I couldn't move. He swiftly stepped up and took my hand. Although he pulled me gently, I stubbed my toe against the top step, almost falling into the water.

He led me down the steps, through the door, and into the pool. My eyes stayed fixed on the water. I heard a different quietness, a friendly calm. The silence played softly in my ears.

"It's a wonderful thing that we have these children joining the church," Howard K. said into the noiselessness. "Kenneth Paul Kramer, do you now openly declare your profession of faith in God?"

My mouth was dry. "I do," I finally said in a low voice. "Do you take Jesus as your personal Lord and Savior?"

"I do," I replied without looking up.

"I now baptize you in the name of the Father" . . . he slowly lowered me back into the cool water . . . "and the Son" . . . my head broke the surface, and the water rushed up my nostrils . . . "and the Holy Ghost." He lifted me from the water and placed a towel over my face. He dried my eyes, mounted the steps, and walked me out of the congregation's sight.

Do you think I knew what I was doing? Did I realize the significance of this act? Not really! I did what was expected of me at that age. I did what the rest of my church friends were doing. I did what my parents wanted me to do. About fitting in, I never had any doubts.

Understand, daughters, that this was a HUGE moment for me. I fully hoped/expected that this ritual act would embody some magical energy that would make me feel differently. Did anything change for me afterward? I did feel happy that I had not made any mistakes during the ceremony. Otherwise, nothing that I noticed changed.

I sensed that by being baptized I was somehow beginning a new connection to Jesus, but I didn't feel any different. In fact, my next thought was about lunch and then the afternoon Phillies game.

Decision

My Delightful Daughters,

Neither of my parents finished high school. In fact, my father wasn't able to complete junior high because he, an only child of a bedridden father, needed to work to support his mother. Neither of my parents, therefore, received much of an education. As a result, while it was always assumed that I would finish high school, a career or college beyond that was never talked about.

My earliest plan was to attend Dobbin's Vocational High School, which specialized in teaching students various trades that would enable them to find employment. As an only child in a relatively poor household, I just assumed that it would be necessary for me to find a job immediately upon graduating high school. But then an event happened which altered the course of my life.

One day, after playing basketball in the junior high school yard, my gym teacher, Mr. Williams, called me into the principal's office. I hadn't done anything wrong so I was a bit curious about why he would want to speak with me.

I walked into the principal's minimally decorated office. He motioned for me to sit down in the chair in front of him.

"Kenny," he asked, smiling at me, "have you thought about which high school you will attend next year?"

"No," I said, honestly.

"Would you tell your mother when you go home that I would like her to come and meet me in my office with you. Ask her if she could come tomorrow afternoon and let me know in the morning."

When my mother came the next afternoon she was as curious as I was about the purpose of the meeting. She had asked me the night before if I had done anything wrong. But I hadn't. In fact, of all of my teachers, I liked

Mr. Williams most. He was always willing to spend extra time with students on the playground.

"Hi, Mrs. Kramer," he said, shaking my mother's hand and offering each of us a seat opposite his. "I'm sure you're wondering why I asked you in to see me. I wanted to talk about where your son is going to attend high school. Have you given this any thought?"

"We have talked a little about whether Kenny would go to Northeast High, which is closest to us, or to Dobbin's Vocational School, but no decision has been reached." My mother replied, anxiously gripping her hands.

"I'd like to make a suggestion for your consideration," Mr. Williams said, suddenly seeming a bit more serious. He leaned forward and looked directly into my mother's eyes. "Would you ever consider sending your son to Central High School?"

We were both more than a little surprised. Central High was an all-boys, college-prep school with reputably high academic standards. It was also the arch-football rival of Northeast High School. On Thanksgiving, the two schools played each other in a traditional game. Since neither my mother nor I had ever considered the remotest possibility that I would go to Central, she replied hesitantly, "We've . . . never thought of it as a possibility."

"Well, I think you should," he replied, leaning back into his chair. "I think Kenny would do very well there. His grades and work habits qualify him. And I would be happy to recommend him. Why don't you think about it and let me know?"

In our fifteen-minute walk home, your grandmother and I discussed this possibility. It certainly would be challenging. It certainly would break new ground. It certainly would open up new opportunities that I had never considered. But could I do it?

"It's your decision, Kenny," my mother finally said. "I'll support you in whatever you want to do."

Central it was. Though somewhat daunting for certain, the challenge excited me. Plus, two of my friends, Eddie Virtue and Bobbie Richards, were going to Central next year with me.

I have often thought back on how different my life might have been had it not been for my gym teacher, Mr. Williams. Going to Central High School exposed me to higher learning, but more importantly it exposed me to other students who were highly motivated to pursue college and careers

I—Formative Years (1941–1963)

beyond. This had never even crossed my mind as the remotest of possibilities, but now all of a sudden, there it was.

When I left junior high school to attend Central high in the fall of 1956 a young fourteen years old, I was tested immediately. My junior high pals, Virtue and Richards, who had agreed to meet me at the Broad Street subway, suddenly dropped out of sight. And I never knew why. And when I saw them in school, they wouldn't talk to me.

I was devastated and more than a little anxious about striking out on my own. When I told my mother what had happened, she suggested asking other boys who I noticed riding the subway if I could join them. The next day I approached Tommy Isadore and Walter Kobiaka, already almost six feet tall, whom I had seen at school and who rode the train at the exact same time that I did.

What a stroke of good fortune it turned out to be, especially getting to know Kobiaka. Why? Because not only did he introduce me to Robert Frost's poetry ("Two roads diverged in a wood, and I-/I took the one less travelled by,/And that has made all the difference") but because he wrote poetry himself. What?! He wrote his own poems! For whatever reason, writing poems was something I attributed to professional writers. And while I don't remember any he wrote, or even if he ever shared any of his poetry with me, the fact that he wrote his own poems intrigued me.

Sports, Sports, Sports

My Spirited Daughters,

I once found a framed second place award certificate for a Junior High 100-yard dash that my father had won. Why did he frame it, I wonder, and why did he keep it? These are questions I never thought to ask him, but it's easy to see, looking back, that my interest in sports came partly from his athleticism.

I could ask myself a similar question: Why did I save my 1959 high school year book all these years? Why did I need this description of myself to remain inscribed and collected?

At present, Ken holds two class records. First, he has grown more than anyone in the class in the last four years (from 5'4" to 6'2"). Second, he has never, in four long and tedious years, though hurricane, blizzard, and PTC strike, been absent from school. Ken had taken full advantage of these records by participating on the JV basketball team, and in all intramurals. An intelligent, hard-working, personable fellow like Ken cannot avoid success.

Who was this "me" I have clung on to for so long?

As a kid, I lived to play. Sport was the only thing that mattered to me. My street uniform, when I was young, never varied: sneakers, jeans, and a polo shirt, with or without a glove, depending on the game being played.

We met at the schoolyard (our playground) to choose up sides and get started. Usually, we played a game using a pimple, a pinky, or a tennis ball, but once in a while we played basketball at the end of the yard, where the only basket (without a net) was planted. When we were not playing a ball game, my friends and I rode bikes. In winter, we would hide behind the cars that were parked near the intersections. Then, unseen by drivers waiting at the stop sign, we would grab ahold of their rear bumpers and be pulled along on our sleds down the street. I never told my mother about this crazy fun.

I — Formative Years (1941–1963)

One day, several of us were playing half ball, which we played with pimple balls cut in half, using a broomstick for a bat. The half pimple ball would be tossed underhand, somewhat like a Frisbee, and soar across an empty street toward a batter, who stood on the pavement opposite the pitcher with his back to a wall. Smack! The hitter smacked the ball.

If the pitcher was able to catch it as it rebounded off the wall, the batter was out. Of course, a batter, once in a while, was able to loft the half ball over the roof for a home run. This action, as great for the batter as it was, usually halted the game until a new ball could be obtained. We must have been around ten years old at the time.

Once, after a just such a homer, the batter who hit it suggested that we go to a local corner grocery store and that I climb over the backyard fence to grab as many empty soda bottles as possible. We would then return to the store to cash in the bottles (which had already been cashed in once) for enough money to buy a new pimple ball. The ball could then be cut in half with a knife to make two half balls.

This was a good plan, except that I was the one designated to climb the chain link fence, to grab the empty soda bottles and lift them over to my accomplice, and then to climb back. Well, just as I was climbing back over the fence, who was walking down 7th Street on her way home from work, in her white cafeteria uniform, but Mom?

"What are you doing?" The truth spurted out of my mouth faster than I was able to climb down the fence. I couldn't lie to her. My accomplice had, of course, sprinted away by now. My mother immediately marched me into the store, empty soda bottles in hand, and made me confess what I had done and pay the owner for the bottles I'd taken. Since I had no money—that, after all, was the reason for the heist—she paid and then took it out of my allowance later.

Never Before

Leila and Yvonne,

Jean Paul Sartre once claimed that we talk in one language and write in another. How simple yet how clarifying this distinction is. A third kind of language, for me, is episodic. I write short dialogue-centric, parabolic episodes of touchstone moments in my life, events, that have continued to influence me. But it's more than that. My writing has to have its own blood in its veins.

My passion for writing began at age seventeen when, in the summer between high school and college. I did something I had never done before. In contrast with my treeless neighborhood, I went to "World's End" Pennsylvania on a camping trip with Teddy from work. The setting was perfect for an inner-city lad like me. It was my very first time camping. Adding to the thrill I already felt, a river running down from a nearby mountain cut along the ridge at one side of the campgrounds.

One afternoon, while Teddy was using his scuba diving equipment, I was hiking along the river up the ridge. I had brought a notebook and a pen. My innocent eyes were waiting for a twist of experience that would inspire me.

At one point in my climb, a large rock, bedded in a low spot of the river's passageway, beckoned to me and I climbed onto it. It offered a fairly comfortable place to be swept into the sound of the river's tumbling. It was a sound to be remembered. That day, the water's gush flowed into a kind of silence, one that turned me away from nature's surprises to somewhere else deeply inward. What I remember from what I wrote are the first lines of a poem that, thankfully, never abused anyone's ears but my mother's.

I — Formative Years (1941–1963)

> As the roaring, rampant, rivulet ran
> Diverted by each ornate stone's span,
> Above in the azure blues of the sky,
> While below looking-clear waters still flow . . .

Fortunately, I can't recall any more of this alliteration-dripping, cliché-infused verse. It was, however, an early advance into what remained, for me, an alien world. Writing the poem opened up a new way of seeing myself. I wasn't just a boy with a ball in my hands. I could imagine. I could write.

But why do I write this story? Certainly, it's not to sum up my life. Too much of my life is not recorded here: unremembered moments, filtered out events, and unimportant memories are left in the drawer.

This book is connected with my death, with wanting to share a few life-memories with intimate family and close friends. I sing my heart out for this beautiful universe, just in case something gets said or written, an experience described, an insight remembered, a breakthrough activated, a question raised, an answer contradicted, that can out-live this life and be useful in a me-less version of "me" when I am gone. Just so.

Girls, as you will come to know, I write every day at the same time and in the same way because I know there'll be a time when I can't write . . . but *I can't not write*. Sitting in my motorized wheel chair at my two-sided desk, sipping organic java, I write to keep alive.

Missed Free Throws

Spirited Girls,

Success took her time. It came, but I'm not sure when. Certainly not when I was an undergrad. Even though I reached the pinnacle of my athletic abilities by unexpectedly playing varsity basketball and baseball, success did not await me in that realm. Strangely enough, it would take a life-altering neurological malady —Multiple Sclerosis —to point me in the direction I needed to take. My athletic motor would be re-directed into academia.

Sophomore year, spring 1960 at the Palestra —Temple University plays against the taller St. Joseph's team. The winner will secure a position in the highly coveted NCAA playoffs, the loser will play in New York's NIT. Then, as today, winning the NCAA tournament was every player's dream. Basketball in the middle of the last century was played not just in another era, but in another world. The athleticism, skill, physical power, and size of the players were drastically different.

I—Formative Years (1941–1963)

The game was scheduled on a Friday evening, and the sports pages in Philadelphia beat the drum throughout the week. The Palestra was sold out. Our tallest man, Russell, was 6'4 ½" tall. St. Joseph's center, Mike Kaminski, was 6'8 ½". So we knew it was going to be difficult under the boards.

As I did all season, I began this most important game on the bench. Usually, at 6'3" and 185 lbs., I was our first "big" man substitute, even though we also had a 6'4 ½" reserve sitting next to me.

My road to becoming Temple's 6th man in my sophomore year is made all the more interesting by the fact that I never played high school basketball. I was always more interested in baseball, even once trying out with the Philadelphia Phillies at Shibe Park. At that time, games were rarely televised, so I became a radio junkie. The 1950s "whiz-kids," as the Phillies

Missed Free Throws

were nicknamed, made it all the way to the World Series, only to be defeated in four straight games by the dreaded New York Yankees.

My "hustle" overcame my lack of such skills as dribbling with my left hand, which, like typing, I never mastered. As a result of a successful second half of the season, I was called into the athletic director's office when the season ended and given a "senatorial scholarship," which covered half of my tuition. It came with a commitment that I would play on the varsity basketball team the next year.

Mission impossible, yet it happened. And now I was playing in the biggest game of my life before a sell-out crowd that included family and friends. During the layup drills, before the game, my adrenaline was gushing so fast that, for the first (and only) time in my life, I dunked the basketball.

The game itself was close. We couldn't really contain their center and they couldn't really stop our guards. Toward the middle of the second half, Coach Harry Litwack called out, "Kenny, go in for Russell." Russell, our tallest player and best defender, had just committed his fourth foul. Nervously, excitedly, I ran to the scorer's table. "Kramer for Russell," I shouted over the crowd noise.

Screaming fans greeted my entry. Before I could worry about anything going wrong, I was racing up and down the court, first on offense, then on defense. When one of our players was fouled, I lined up on the foul line next to their big center. My teammate missed his free throw; the ball hit the back of the rim, bounced on an arc that eluded their center's reach and fell into my hands. I jumped again and put the ball back into the basket. Yelling and screaming filled my years.

When the coach put Russell back in the game with a few minutes remaining, he left me in. Having scored yet another goal, I was feeling as if I belonged with the other starters. Then the play that helped decide the outcome of the game happened, and it happened to me.

Hustle is necessary. Yes. So, too, is the ability to shoot foul shots under pressure before thousands of screaming fans. In the last seconds of the game, with the score tied, I received a pass at the top of the circle. Suddenly, I saw a lane open up to the basket and dribbled with my right hand on a straight line. Just as I jumped, thinking I would lay the ball into the basket, just as I released the ball from my fingertips, their 6'8 ½" center, whom I didn't see, leapt over and blocked my shot. In the process, however, he fouled me. Two shots.

I—Formative Years (1941–1963)

"Time out," their coach yelled. In the huddle, Coach Litwack tried to calm me down. The noise only intensified my nervousness. Everyone was standing. Everyone was watching everything I did. And I was aware of it all. There was no place to hide. Not that I wanted to hide, I wanted to disappear. So much depended on what I did.

Taking my position behind the foul line, arranging my feet in a parallel fashion, equidistant behind the stripe, I bounced the ball several times, trying unsuccessfully to get comfortable. Everything felt slightly out of sync. The ball never quite felt right in my hand. I bent my knees and released the ball. My first shot bounced off the back rim and fell away from the basket. Cheering and groaning filled my ears. I only needed to make one shot.

"What if I miss?" I thought. With everyone standing, yelling, I bent my knees and pushed up the second time. The shot was straight, except not long enough. This time it bounced off the front rim and fell away from the basket. It didn't matter that in the overtime period, other players made similar mistakes. We lost. This defining moment effectively ended my basketball career.

You may wonder why, after all these years, there is so much detail in this letter to you girls. Certainly, I'm not bragging here. No. Deeper, however, is the fact that in less than a decade, I would discover I could never play basketball again. I want you to be able to really picture it—your papa, young and fearless, tan and fit, running furiously up and down the court—a picture of youthful health.

And then . . .

On First Meeting Eliot and Buber

My Intellectual Daughters,

I was not a stellar student. With a fresh crew cut, buttoned shirt (clean and pressed), and beige khakis, I showed up at my Temple classes more eager than intellectually ready. Although I went to Central High, sports always came first. It was as if college classes were for everyone else but not me.

In my Sophomore year at Temple in an English Literature class, though, I seriously encountered poets and poetry for the first time like —W.B. Yeats' "The Wild Swans at Coole," Wallace Stevens' "Anecdote of the Jar." Emily Dickinson's "I Heard a Fly Buzz When I Died," and W.C. Williams' "Red wheel barrow/glazed with rain/water/beside the white/chickens." But in this beauteous swarm of modern British and American poetry, it was T.S. Eliot whose words most deeply addressed who I was (and wasn't) at the time.

I have never forgotten T.S. Eliot's poem "The Lovesong of J. Alfred Prufrock" with its intriguingly jaded invitation:

> Let us go then, you and I,
>
> When the evening is spread out against the sky
>
> Like a patient etherized
>
> Upon a table.

I was immediately grasped by Eliot's image of a man who "Measured out [his] life with/Coffee spoons," whose overwhelming question still rings out with undiminished freshness and audacity: "Do I dare/Disturb the universe?" I still recall an undergraduate professor highlighting the lines, "I should have been a pair of ragged claws/Scuttling across the floors of silent seas." As it must be for many of Eliot's readers, I was captured by the chilling ripening delightfulness of these images. I felt myself rising to meet the music of the poetry and longing for a context to better understand it.

I — Formative Years (1941–1963)

Then, in my final undergraduate semester, I decided to audit a Western Philosophy course. This way of using language to communicate ideas was brand new to me. Thinking philosophically, I learned in that class to reset my own thinking, and this skill served me throughout graduate school and on into my teaching career.

I learned, in particular, not to be frightened by long, convoluted sentences, but to instead find and focus the sentence and then trace its nuances, its turns, flips, and its associations. Had I not learned this mode of reading, I would never have been able to understand the meanings of Martin Buber's ideas that "the basic meaning of human existence is person with person" and that "all real living is encounter."

One day in philosophy class, the professor discussed Martin Buber, a German-Jewish philosopher of "I-Thou" dialogue and said that, for Buber, genuine dialogue (present, direct, and two-sided) existed not only between people but also between people and nature.

He then read from a passage in Buber's classic *I and Thou* in which Buber speaks of entering into an I-Thou relationship with a tree — a tree! While we normally relate to trees as objects of our perception, as a problem for builders, or as a source of wood, there is another way to know a tree: as a Thou, as a unique other. The professor then read: "Everything belonging to the tree, its form and structure, its colors and chemical composition, its intercourse with the elements and with the stars, are all present in a single whole."

I never forgot that. How could I? No one in my life had talked about being addressed by a tree. Five years later, I would return to Temple (after studying theology and teaching for a year) to begin my PhD in Religion and Literature. And who turned out to be my major professor? Maurice Friedman. And who was Maurice Friedman? It was Maurice Friedman who almost single-handedly introduced the work of Martin Buber to the United States with his 1955 book, *Martin Buber: The Life of Dialogue* and with his translations of many of Buber's books and articles.

How could I possibly ever suspect that Buber and Eliot — who actually met once in London — would become such stellar intellectual/spiritual role models for me. If ever there was a conversation I would have wished to join, it would have been theirs. I'd listen for:

How Buber responded to Eliot's seminal poem, *The Four Quartets*.
How Eliot responded to Buber's seminal work, *I and Thou*.

On First Meeting Eliot and Buber

Unfortunately, all that remains to know is a letter that T.S. Eliot wrote to Friedman about their meeting. In the one comment that remains between these men, T.S. Eliot remarks, "I got the strong impression that I was in the company of a great man. There are only a very few men of those whom I have met in my lifetime, whose presence has given me that feeling."

Setting Forth

Dear Yvonne and Leila,

Who knew?

It took looking back over my shoulder to recognize how the playful innocence of my first twenty-one years prepared me to set forth confidently on the next stage of my life. I was neither stressed out nor screwed up. In fact, I was excited to wake up each day. When I thought about it, which wasn't often, I was amazed by how many new things were unfolding around me.

I was set forth from birth into the unknown distance, by my untraveled parents, to maintain a common sense presence no matter where I was. After my father traded our radio-less, blue '41 Chevy Sedan for a brand new white Ford Falcon with an AM radio, he shocked me by saying, "Your mother and I have decided to give you the car to use while you're at theological school." With that, he handed me the keys.

So I set forth to discover, and to become at home with, that which creates, that which reveals, and that which redeems us.

I set forth with a powerful longing to create something new, and in the process realized the inestimable value of finding my own way.

Though I was not always certain where I was headed, I was given the freedom to do as I saw fit. All I knew was to follow my common sense. Common sense —that which is most reasonable —made what I was doing (even though it was different from anything I had done before) okay.

How could I have known that after leaving home at twenty-one (never to return), I would march in civil rights protests in Williamston, North Carolina, spend a summer hitch-hiking through Europe, sing in a folk trio, be excused from all classes to study for two years in a special studies program at Andover Newton, and then go on to study for a master's degree at Yale Divinity School, where I would receive an invitation that would turn the rest of my life around.

Setting Forth

My wish for you girls is that you will be blessed with a bucket full of common sense, and that a door will open for you to see an ancestor reappear in waiting words.

II

Leaving Home
(1963–1974)

Andover Newton

Honestly, Leila and Yvonne, let's face it:

I spent three years at Andover Newton (just outside of Boston) because a) there was nowhere else to go b) it gained me a four-D exemption from the Vietnam fiasco c) I didn't have the grades necessary for grad school in English literature d) it was free and e)I admit, I was curious to know more about the ultimate mystery of the Universe.

But no sooner did I arrive, filled with questions about who Jesus really was and what he meant when he spoke in parables, I was confronted with an existential challenge:

"You've never really suffered, Ken," John Rutland said in one of our all-night cram sessions in my first year at theological school. John was a tall, twenty-two year-old, thin Southerner who arrived at Andover Newton at the same time I did. His remark—which I immediately dismissed—came in response to my disbelief that an unconditionally loving God could punish someone eternally. He was right, of course —I hadn't really suffered, certainly not like he had. Just three years later, John put a bullet in his head.

I had no resources, at the time, to begin to imagine why a bright young man would terminate his life. No. It seemed so wrong, yet he was right about me. I had never really suffered.

To begin my studies, I brought with me to Andover Newton a newly purchased large, black, Sears & Roebucks stereo record player and about a dozen vinyl records. Of course, there was Bob Dylan, Peter Paul and Mary, and The Mamas and the Papas, along with Ray Charles, Dave Brubeck, and Ray Mancini; I also brought Tchaikovsky's "1812 Overture" (I loved the cannons firing at the end) and the Mormon Tabernacle Choir for inspiration.

Each Sunday morning and afternoon, I worked at First Baptist Church in Melrose in fulfillment of my fieldwork assignment. In the evening, I drove into Copley Square and attended Trinity Episcopal Church, which

II—Leaving Home (1963–1974)

gave way from a plain white building both inside and out to a cathedral-like cavernous edifice with red carpets, ornate statuary and stained glass windows. The main attraction at Trinity Episcopal, for me, was the Reverend Theodor Parker Ferris, who climbed the stairs to a brass eagle lectern to deliver his homily. It was there that I first heard eloquent sermons in which theology and poetry collided (as if God really does belong to everything He's made), and I took them back to my room with me, since copies were made freely at the front door.

At Andover Newton, my encounter with critical scholarship and liberal thinking continued to rearrange my faith. Theologians like Paul Tillich taught that faith was impossible without doubt; not skeptical doubt, but existential doubt. Skeptical doubt is what you girls may have experienced when preparing for a difficult exam—the fear and insecurity stemming from doubt over whether or not you know enough. Existential doubt, on the other hand, is in the realm of trust, faith, or belief about your place in the world. It has to do with your ordinary, everyday existence.

It didn't matter to me, at that point, that my fellow seminarian Bill, from Dallas, couldn't accept Tillich's God. Standing outside the chapel one day, he said to me, "But Ken, Tillich's God is not personal."

There I also encountered: Nels Ferre, a professor of systematic theology, whose spontaneous laughing in his lectures and chapel sermons kept our attention riveted on his "God is *agape*" theology, and Harvey Cox, a professor of social ethics who inspired me to travel with other theological students to Williamston, North Carolina to participate in the Civil Rights marches there.

Each of us spent a week living with an African-American family, eating at their tables, discussing their fears and concerns, and sharing our support for them. Honestly, the main thing I brought back from this brief experience was the knowledge of some of the freedom songs we sang each day with the families in church. Songs like "Ain't Gonna Let Nobody Turn Me 'Round," and "Oooh, Freedom," and "I'm On My Way to Freedom Land," and "This Little Light of Mine."

Aside from Paul Tillich's theology, I was most impressed with Rudolph Bultmann's de-mythologizing of the New Testament. It was Bultmann who said, "Myth does not want to be interpreted in cosmological terms but in anthropological terms or, better, in existentialist terms." This offered me a hermeneutical tool that severely challenged the Philadelphia Baptist image of a white Jesus. Literalism, be gone!

Andover Newton

By the time I completed Andover Newton Theological School, not only did I still not know where I'd end up (not as a Baptist preacher, that was certain), but many of my conservative beliefs had shifted. When I re-read a poem today that I wrote while a student there, it reminds me of how naïve I was:

"but Prophecy would have him"

Though drunk inside his head with peace,
and damned by brotherhood,
he reaches in word for feet
to stand where Prophets stood.

And when he happens to stumble,
while turning inside out,
his bumptious friends insouciantly flay:
"FOOL!" they shout.

His country walks behind him,
echoing the churchified fear
of all the bygone voices,
handicapped, without an ear.

He wears his shoe-soles empty
giving wings to the slow —
an apocalyptic witness
that fire will eat the snow.

And all the while his journey,
too inconvenient to spell,
sails the pool of agony
inside his inside well.

II—Leaving Home (1963-1974)

> How long go on, how long ...
> I do not know to tell,
> but Prophecy would have him
> outlast the hypertrophy of Hell.

"Of what value were those three years?" you ask.

It's always about whom you meet (especially those who remain life-friends) and what you learn (which provides a stepping stone to the next learning experience).

Andover Newton taught me that my future did not lie in becoming a Baptist preacher, a theologian or even a member of the Protestant tradition. Rather, it was about more learning, more studying, and more schooling. It was about taking the next step toward the interdisciplinary study (and, as I would soon discover, teaching) of religion and literature.

"The Travesty"

My Adventurous Girls,

You've heard a lot about Robert Morgan over the years and you certainly remember his painting, which he gave me, of the disgruntled Swami. The staggering humor of this piece hung for years on our bathroom wall for all to see. Look at his mouth, frown, and arms. Holy man, he aint!

I first met Morgan at Andover Newton about 50 years ago and we have been good friends since then —he, a professor, poet, art historian, painter, curator, writer, international lecturer; me, a religious historian, a professor, writer, and a single parent.

After I finished my first year of theological school, influenced by Jack Kerouac's *On The Road*, I decided to spend the summer of '64 hitchhiking through Europe to reach Jerusalem. I showed up at the LaGuardia International airport with a round-trip ticket to Amsterdam: early, over-packed, scared with excitement, a lonely and nervous explorer. How happy I was when, who showed up in the departure lounge with a ticket to Amsterdam, too, but Robert Morgan.

"Morges" started Andover Newton Theological School when I did, but dropped out after enduring, what he called in a booklet he wrote describing his experience, "The Travesty." In it, he withheld nothing. He fired out against the intolerable hierarchy of theological oppression that rejected his unique creativity.

"Morgan!" I yelled enthusiastically, spotting him on the other side of the gate.

"Kramer!"

We dropped everything and hugged each other on the spot.

"Where you goin'?"

"Where YOU goin'?"

II—Leaving Home (1963–1974)

The bones in my body began singing like they had once done when we were driving in his green VW bug along Storrow Drive by the Charles River. Uninebriated, as he drove, he strummed his guitar while singing folk and civil rights songs with me. It was one of those out-of-body-with-pure-joy moments. He was a strummin' and a laughin' and a singin' fool, but not without me.

"Freedom, freedom" we had bellowed forth. "Freedom."

Oh, if only THAT moment could have been videotaped —I'd want it played for you girls when it's my time to go.

Morgan was visiting European art museums to see the master works (and the not so masterly works) in their own environment. What I was up to, I really didn't know, and I couldn't verbalize it. There was this need to step forth into the unknown on my own. It was time to vacate the familiar and navigate my way to historic sites and culture-shaping places.

For the first time in my life, I was flooded by different cultures, different languages, and most of all, different ways of looking at America and at myself. In the heart of Europe, an American can sense a difference between Europeans and oneself. It seemed to me that Europeans, with their longer history, didn't take ownership of their living spaces as we do. They seemed content to be tenants of the earth.

While Morgan and I went our separate ways after spending time in Amsterdam, we've remained good friends to this day, each deeply respecting the work of the other. Over the years, we continued to maintain a hyper-spirited (and, for me, often herbally-enhanced) slew of letters. The letters still fill the extra-large, lower right-hand drawer in my desk. Morgan tells me that he still has his collection of the letters as well. Beyond the joy each of us experienced sending and receiving them, each of us was also experimenting with words, learning when to use which ones and how. Crooked phrases and sentences poured out.

Toward the end of the last century, Morgan encouraged me to start thinking of this book by suggesting:

> Dear Ken,
>
> The focus of your book should be—at a time when religions seem to be what is separating humankind from one another—the contiguity between various religions; but what would make your book special is your personal journey from being raised a Protestant, to being married to a Jewish wife, to Zen Buddhism, to [Benedictine]

"The Travesty"

Catholicism, to Buber in a more humanistic way, rather than simply becoming an ideologue.

Robert

Aside from being taken completely off guard by his structuring of my life, I experienced two strong reactions on reading this. The first was the realization that the structural integrity of the first three stages of my interreligious journey—Baptist, Zen Buddhist, Catholic—has led me to the present moment. The reasons behind my passage through these stages, I realized over the next few days, might actually be of some interest to one who is pursuing and following on different spiritual teachings or practices.

Next, not only "why" but also "how" I did what I did began to ferment in my memory. The more I ruminated on Robert's suggestion, the more I retraced the steps leading to where I now stand. The more I recognized that the context in which this journey took on its deepest significance—at least for me—was not defined by the differences between various religious traditions but by the division within each of them. I knew it needed to be written.

Yale's Unexpected Calling

My Ever-Aspiring Daughters,

Since I did not want to enter the Baptist ministry (to the great chagrin of my father), it was an easy choice for me to enter Yale Divinity School, where I would study for a Master of Sacred Theology (STM). This choice was made even easier by the fact that my tuition at Yale was waived. Admittedly, I also couldn't resist the thought of the name of "Yale" appearing on my vitae.

But what then?

While it didn't take long for me to realize that courses at Yale Divinity offered more of the same Christ-o-centric material that I had become accustomed to in my graduate training, the courses I took in the graduate English Studies department, especially with Cleanth Brooks, opened up new intellectual vistas for me.

Professor Brooks spent weeks taking students on a tour through each of Eliot's the *Four Quartets*. I still have the notes I took in his class on Eliot's complete poems and plays, some of which I would later use when writing my dissertation on the poem.

One evening after an intermural basketball game, the unexpected happened. A brand new door opened. A fellow seminarian, Tom Beason asked me out of the blue: "Would you be interested in spending a year at my alma mater Saint Andrews Presbyterian College to teach English Literature and Christianity and Culture?"

What?!

I had never conceived of myself as a University teacher. Never. Yet, as soon as Tom presented this possibility, I immediately knew that it was the next right thing for me. How I knew, I can't say. As soon as a doubt-generating-panic knifed its way through me, it passed, and courage replaced it.

What happened? A "calling," a "summoning," addressed me in the depths of my being. It wasn't like Isaiah or Jeremiah's prophetic calls. They saw visions, heard voices, were touched on the lips by the celestial messenger, and were commissioned to speak in the name of the Lord. I was leaving that life behind. Instead, I was filled with a deep urging that seemed to be rising from the world itself, and this new possibility hit me with a powerful energy. It would open the door to my life's vocation.

Teaching—sharing what I know with and learning from engaged students—became, as Confucius said in his *Analects*, a "Great Joy." Soon, I would come to know that's where I belonged.

Soon, I would come to taste the fruits of teaching, especially when teaching does not limit itself to transmitting information but is entered into with a spirit of trust in the back-and-forth process of dialogue.

"Calling," is a word that I would use in your upbringing, is a word I learned in Seminary and carried over into life. When you asked me: "How did you know that teaching was what you wanted to do," I'd respond, "Because I was called to it!" And when you asked, Leila, "By what?" I always answered, "By the Universe." That was the best answer I could give you. "It's the Universe calling you into the way that you should go."

Did I have any fear? Anxieties, yes, but I never once thought of rejecting this invitation. I knew it was the right thing to do even though I also knew I didn't know what I was doing. I wonder if you girls can imagine the excited anxiety that was pulsing through me. Have either of you ever had an unexpected calling of your own?

Leila, I remember when you were at the University of Michigan and accepted an invitation to be a TA in a completely different department from what you had ever studied. That's far more daunting than what I did! And Yvonne, wasn't this true for you when you got your first job without fully being sure what was expected of you? I am so proud of you both!

First Class: First Day

My Brilliant Girls,

What happened next caused me to feel as if my life had just begun. The first real Southerner I met, Jim Smith, would become my roommate in the second story of Ms. Parker's two-story house in Laurinburg, North Carolina. He was a tall, thin, fifth-year, long distance runner at Saint Andrews. Jim never forgot our first meeting:

> I was upstairs when Ken arrived at the house. I turned to go downstairs, as he began to walk up. There he was, and in one of those rare moments in life it was so strong that I knew I saw someone, in an instant, who would be a friend. That year we ate boxes and boxes of the new cereal called Life, beat all the neighborhood kids in sandlot football, shared many a discussion on whether whole wheat bread was better than white. A boy from Alabama, and a man from Philadelphia, we talked about race, religion, life from different worlds. An unlikely pair . . .

He was the first person to call me by my last name in a way and with a tone and accent that completely complimented me. "Kramer," he said with a Georgian smile wrapped around the sound. "Kramer, let's go." He always wanted to do, to travel, to see, to play. It must have been his accent sliding around the curves of the letters spelling "Kramer" that tickled me so.

All of a sudden, it was time. I'd spent the summer of 1967 preparing to teach for the first time by re-reading the major British and American poets. I worked toward creating a master narrative for the course, integrating poets such as Auden, Yeats, Eliot, Stevens, Cummings, and William Carlos Williams.

Yet, in all of this intellectual preparation, I left out an essential element — my manner of teaching (my style, my methods, and my techniques). I had never been taught to teach, and I had never read a book on *how* to

First Class: First Day

teach. Just as the problem of how to take a picture never occurred to me before I took my first picture, the question of how to teach had never entered my mind.

Yet, with four years of undergrad English Lit and four years of theological training under my belt, I stepped in, if a bit quixotically, with a fresh haircut and a new shirt.

It couldn't have been more ideal. Early September, North Carolina; a small private college set on blue-green acres in a sleepy little city forty-five minutes from Chapel Hill; less than a thousand respectful, well-mannered Southerners riding the maturity train on the parents' dime under manicured-trees. I was not afraid of the number of students that would show up. I had played basketball before crowds of ten thousand fans; I had preached before several hundred congregants at once; in seminary, I had sung Peter, Paul and Mary's "If I Had a Hammer" to Pete Seager's "We Shall Overcome" in a folk trio in high school auditoriums.

It wasn't being in front of many students that prompted my nervousness. It was not knowing what questions they might ask. It was not knowing what questions they might ask, and the possibility of not knowing how to answer a specific question. Would my authority crumble if that might happen?

Into a "Modern British and American Poetry" class of twenty-five freshman and sophomores I walked, decked out in sports jacket and tie and carrying pages and pages of newly typed notes and books of poetry littered with markings. First, I looked up to make eye-contact, stranger-to-stranger, with the students.

Next, as the new teacher on the block, I removed my sports jacket to present myself less formally. Then, looking at the students (as if there should be no dead air), I said: "Phewph!" (with a slightly over-exaggerated expression of relief). "Ahh, that's much better." Laughter followed.

The unintended dramatic playfulness of that first pre-teaching gesture in that small southern college classroom awakened something buried in me.

I followed that laughter with a spontaneous first question: "Any questions?" This time the laughter was a little louder, a little longer.

Feeling much more relaxed at and home, I told them who I was, where I had studied, and why I was so interested in the course material.

"Oh," interrupting myself, "wait a minute! I forgot what's really important here." Pause. "Moi," I said, "Me!"

II—Leaving Home (1963–1974)

More laughter.

Instinctively, while they were focused on the humor in the situation, I segued into announcing the class content, required readings, grading, and office hours.

I began to feel more emboldened and dropped any pretense that I was anyone other than, simply, myself.

Thus it began—my first laughter-infused class presentation. While it took years to hone the performance art I had stumbled into at that first class, I walked away elevated, realizing how natural the dialogic process of teaching (talking, listening, questioning, and responding) was for me. And the more laughter, the better.

Plus, they took notes on what I was saying!

Looking back on the first few weeks of teaching (and I don't even know if it took that long), I was totally hooked. This, this performance art with a little improv sprinkled in, was *it* for me. What could be more joyous than engaging a student (or a few students) who are deeply interested in the class material and deeply attentive to what's being said? How wonderful when someone lights up, when someone gets the opportunity to figure out what has been questionable for them.

I was flushed with the joy/action/power of teaching. It was intoxicating. I felt like a conductor standing in front of an orchestra, reaching out to reveal previously-unheard sounds.

From the beginning, the process called me to create new ways of teaching, new ways of making this educational music. I was fortunate, therefore, to grow into the teachers' role believing that learning should be dialogical.

No matter where it happened, no matter who was teaching, no matter who was listening, when dialogue connected teachers, students, and material, magic could, if only briefly, overtake the situation. Real learning takes place when we are changed.

I became so overtaken that I immediately applied to three universities to begin PhD studies the following year. I was on my way "to the freedom land."

This improvisational joy, this irresistible happiness, trumped all my uncertainties about the future. What uncertainties? Like removing an affirming letter from its sealed envelope, all my doubts were ripped apart. It wasn't that I had found my vocation. No. My vocation had found itself in me. And, in me, it found an adventurous partner—one ready, willing, and able to proceed no matter what.

Finding Out

My Loving Daughters,

Writing this reminds me of how a primary scenario of my life is one of "coming out" as someone with MS, declaring and disclosing its limitations on me without shame. This, though, was one of the most difficult things for me to do—to own up to the fact that this mysterious disease was working its way in and through my body with nothing known that I could do about it. As you have come to learn, I have not always been open to discussing effects produced by my MS—its mitigations, limitations, and medication-caused weaknesses.

I was diagnosed at age twenty-six, while I was teaching at St. Andrews Presbyterian College. It frightened me, and yet I didn't know enough about its effects to really be terrified. It would only be later, when the physical effects became obvious to others, that I had to drop the mask I was using to hide it. Of course, as I'm pretty sure must be the case for many MSers, after my diagnosis, irregular episodes in my previous life came to make more sense.

At ten-years-old, my mother was going with me to watch me race at the YMCA swimming pool. I was a good swimmer. I was ready. It was the first time she would ever see me perform. The race began with me in the lead. Half way, I was still winning. Three quarters, still. But as soon as I approached the finish wall, my legs went numb. I lost. I was crushed. Devastated. What happened?

Then, at fifteen, I had a tryout with the high school JV football team, first for the fullback position. The first hand-off I received, I was immediately hit hard by a linebacker while I was still in the backfield. That did it for full-back. No problem, I thought. I'll try out to become the kicker. But just as I attempted to kick the football, for my first kick, my leg went dead. What happened?

II—LEAVING HOME (1963–1974)

Then, at twenty-three, while playing a pickup basketball game at Andover Newton Theological School, both of my legs went numb and it was difficult, thereafter, for me to jump. The "What happened?" question didn't usually last long because, within a week, the numbness would disappear.

When an optometrist discovered retrobulber optic neuritis (yikes!) in my right eye, I was sent to the Duke University hospital where I was given a spinal tap. I had no idea that anything was wrong. Without thinking, I brought books, prepared lesson plans, and graded papers. Of course, I got friendly with the attractive nurses. Even sitting in the doctor's office afterward, I was clueless, but he had a difficult time looking into my eyes.

Peering at me from behind a large brown desk, he asked, "Do you know what you have?"

How the hell would I know? I thought to myself. *I'm here to find out.* "No," I said. "What?"

When he told me, "Mr. Kramer . . . you have Multiple Sclerosis," I looked at him with a blank stare. What was that? "It's an auto-immune disease about which we don't know very much," he said. This was my twenty-six year old reaction: I was happier to remain an innocent intellectual than an informed knower.

When I told my parents, my father said nothing (that I remember), even though his father had died in bed as a result of an unknown (at the time) neurological illness. Mother was upset. "Is there anything you can do, Kenneth?" she asked me, ready to do anything necessary.

"Nothing, but eat well, don't smoke, exercise, and get lots of rest."

Imagine, my girls, finding out you had a serious disease that could kill you about which there's not that much information available (even to this day).

I would later find out that in autoimmune diseases (like type 1 diabetes, lupus, and ALS), the body attacks its own healthy tissues. In my case, these tissues are the myelin sheaths coating the nerves along which brain signals are transmitted to my muscles. The cause is unknown.

Who am I kidding? The next time I stepped onto a basketball court, I caught the ball with my chest instead of my hands. I had lost depth perception for objects speeding toward me. I realized again (as I had when I was not selected in a tryout for the Philadelphia Phillies) that I would dedicate myself to intellectual and spiritual pursuits, to walking with poets and philosophers instead of athletes.

Finding Out

The wild glee, the happy cheer, the laughing freedom of my innocence still confronted the howling storm of the unnerving experience of this disease. I had come face-to-face with William Blake's two contrary states of the human soul: innocence and experience. Each existed within me. Each tried to gain the upper hand. I had zero tools at the time to navigate between them.

Can you imagine the fear and anxiety that caught in my throat? I did not like the prospect of receiving pity. I did not want to be seen as weak . . . to be labeled with the dreaded word, *disabled*. I wanted to remain strong and vibrant in other people's eyes, and it was pity that I was rejecting, before it ever happened. And so, I buried any and all emotion that I had, and never talked about it. My innocence was smashed open, though it soon was replaced with a trust in life as it was given to me.

What followed discovering that I had MS, or, rather, that MS had me? Before personal computers and smart phones, it was easy to dodge this problem and dismiss it. I was both clueless about what it was and uninterested in doing the research to learning more. After all, aside from losing a bit of athletic ability, nothing really seemed to change. What did change, however, was my most immediate future—from living alone to sharing my life with Joanne.

"I'd Like to Get to Know You"

Dear Sweethearts,

The clouds in my eyes were about to disappear. The summer after I graduated from Yale, I met a long wavy-haired blonde in the library where I was preparing my fall courses for St. Andrews Presbyterian College. Having never taught before, I was, of course, overly preparing. In the middle of my work, I looked up and saw her. Why does initial physical attraction happen the way it does—immediate, devastatingly certain, captivating?

In my case, I was looking at a beautifully tanned girl whose tightly fitting beige blouse was completely filled. Immediately, I wanted to see her naked. The wavy-blonde's blouse-filling breasts stopped me dead. She stood up in her short skirt.

Oh *yes*. And oh no, she was leaving and I was totally without a pick-up line.

When she walked up to the front desk to check out her books (I discovered later that she was spending the summer working for a grad professor), I frantically rehearsed a few opening lines. But they were lame and lamer. Then she left the library.

Shit! Jumping out of my brain and with no idea of what to do or say, I leaped up from my chair, and ran for the door, and, not seeing her, started down the hall. She wasn't there. I turned and saw her standing just outside the library door reading announcements on the wallboard. Like a roadrunner, I stopped, reversed direction, then calmly walked to a spot beside her.

"I'd like to get to know you!" I blurted, unthinkingly.

Surprised, she smiled and asked, "What did you have in mind?" What was she looking at? A six-foot three-inch brown haired, blue eyed, Yale grad, who was on the verge of college teaching. A good-looking package, I would think. I had an appealing smile, and a soft mouth. In fact, she may have thought—rightly so—that I was not all that experienced with

"I'd Like to Get to Know You"

women. Just as I thought—wrongly so—that she was not all that experienced with men.

In that moment, I said, "How about this Saturday?"

A week before, I had taken a road trip to San Francisco with a Yale graduate student whose uncle owned a motel overlooking the city. The first evening after we arrived, as we were sitting poolside looking out at the shimmering lights, a stranger walked up and offered us a joint.

Here it was. At twenty-six, I had no experience with marijuana, but I had heard much about its powerful effects. "Why not?" I said. As I was laying down on my back, inhaling and exhaling while staring at the night sky, suddenly "Light My Fire" by The Doors came over the airwaves. Yes! Yes! Yes! The night was set ablaze.

Staring into the face of this amazingly exquisite human being a week later, warmth flushed over me, and all I could hear in my head was The Doors yelling "Come on baby light my fire, tryin' to set the night on FIRE!"

I have no idea what happened next except that I walked away with a "yes" and her phone number. Her name was Joanne Fodor. Oh, and one other thing. I didn't just *walk* away. I skipped away, with raging joy. Meeting a beautiful stranger who agrees to see you again, agrees to spend time with you, to enter into an untold future with *you*—wow! At least, that's how I was picturing it.

Her sweet, twenty-year-old innocence turned out to be more experienced than I was at twenty-seven. It didn't take long before we agreed to stay together. Although I would be in North Carolina teaching while she would be enrolled in an all-girls college in Pennsylvania, we visited back and forth. I knew immediately that I would propose. On her first visit, and thereafter, we had sex (and I know you won't believe me, but I was a twenty-seven year old virgin at the time). Because I was still a brainwashed Baptist, I was influenced by Baptist propaganda that people who had sex were either married or going to become married. The next summer, we were.

Happily, as a married couple, we took up residence in the graduate student apartments at Temple University in Philadelphia. There, Joanne completed her undergraduate degree and I began my PhD.

I was also on the verge of another major life shift, this one substituting one religion, and one spiritual figure, for another.

Temple University Professors

Beautiful Daughters,

What followed a year of teaching and meeting Joanne was a series of landscape shifts, some more seismic than others. The first was graduate school.

In the fall of 1968, newly married, I arrived back at Temple University to begin my PhD work in religious studies. My interest in the field of religion and literature had become my intellectual stand. I was ready to soak in everything I needed to become the teacher I always wished I'd had, one who was able to reshape the traditional power dynamics between teacher and student.

The department chairman, Bernard Phillips, the Zen professor, Richard DeMartino, and my dissertation advisor and Buber scholar, Maurice Friedman, each addressed the question of how one becomes authentically human.

Bernard Phillips opened me to the world of religions and taught me to balance the teachings of Lao Tzu and Confucius.

Richard DeMartino challenged me to the core with his presentation of Kyoto Rinzai Zen Buddhism by asking, "What do you do when whatever you do doesn't work?" Through the lens of Rinzai Zen, he offered perfectly lucid, non-dualistic answers that pointed to self-awakening from dualistic consciousness to non-dualistic consciousness—that is, awakening to awakening itself.

Maurice Friedman introduced me to Martin Buber's life of dialogue (which became the ground that supported my intellectual and spiritual life) and whose own philosophy was centered on concepts like the "human image" and "touchstones of reality." Friedman, through the lens of relational spirituality, spoke of accepting, affirming, and confirming the other as one's partner in genuine dialogue, even when disagreeing.

Girls, I apologize if what follows remains unintelligible. I thought of leaving it out, but I know you've heard some of it before. If you're interested, I would love nothing more than to discuss it with you.

Phillips' "Let That Dilemma Be Your Way"

My first glimpse of Bernard Phillips was a fleeting one. Unbeknownst to him, I was working on a paper for an undergraduate course, "The Bible as Literature." My research took me to the old theological library. There, in a small rectangular reading room, surrounded on three sides by stacks of books, I sat afternoon after afternoon taking notes on the book of Ecclesiastes.

Above me on three sides of the room was a walkway with a railing open to the reading room below. Almost each day, around the same time, a bearded professor made his way from one room to another. I didn't know who he was (I only discovered as a graduate student half a dozen years later that it was Bernard Phillips). Yet, there was something about his demeanor, his gait, and his look that held my attention.

My spiritual life and intellectual attitudes were profoundly reshaped by Dr. Phillips. How? Because he was able to flow so easily between and within the world's living classical religious traditions to the extent that he was, or had been at one time or another, a practitioner of Judaism, Hinduism, Buddhism, and Sufism. I remember him with his shirtsleeves rolled up, his tie loosened, and his curly hair slightly unkempt. One day in the midst of a lecture on Zen Buddhism, Phillips said regarding Jesus, "This is *the* question that a Zen Buddhist asks: When Jesus says, 'I am', who is the 'I' who says, 'I am'? The Buddhist would answer that Jesus can only be referring to the 'I' who is '*not* I', what Nishida called 'absolutely contradictory self-identity.'"

What he said hit me hard, sunk deep, and troubled me. This was not the Jesus of Christian theology I had studied and was used to.

"But what is Zen," I continued asking myself. The very thing I could not grasp was the very thing that had taken hold of me and would not let go. It didn't help—or did it?—that Professor Phillips said in another class:

Phillips' "Let That Dilemma Be Your Way"

There are really four types of Zen. The first is Zen as a school within Mahayana Buddhism, alongside other schools such as Pure Land. The second form of Zen is Zen as the heart, or root source of all schools of Buddhism. The third form is Zen is the heart, or true source of *all* great religions. The fourth form might be called no-Zen Zen, the Zen beyond all forms, true Nothingness beyond all religions. When Zen in this sense is fully concretized, there is no longer anything to be called Zen. The uniqueness of Zen is that when it is fully realized, it bows out of being. When one is in harmony with self and world, there is no path, no religion, no Zen, just life.

But I still didn't have any idea what Zen was. Or perhaps I had too many ideas. But who was I?

One day, Phillips told a story that continues to live with me as a touchstone moment that I have passed along both in my teaching and in parenting you girls. The story is about his encounter with a renowned Zen master that happened in a small café in Tokyo. Phillips had been in Japan practicing Zen for several months, and he was eager to meet with this Zen master Shin'ichi Hisamatsu who, like himself, was also a professor of religions.

As they sat, two cups of tea also sat facing each other silently on the table. From the wordless depths, Phillips spoke: "I know that who I am now (sitting in front of you) is not my *true* self. And I know that you are your true self. Yet I know that you cannot tell me who my true self is. So I face a dilemma."

Without hesitation, and with complete assurance, Hisamatsu replied: "Let that dilemma be your way!" The insight-upon-insight embedded in this response, shared long before I was able to practice it, severely weakened the underpinnings of my Baptist beliefs. Instead of always and only taking your dilemmas to Jesus, as Baptist tradition teaches, Hisamatsu and Phillips made me realize that the responsibility for my dilemmas is my own.

Since I had already completed a year of teaching in North Carolina, and because gaining teaching experience was a part of our degree work, I was appointed next as a teaching assistant. A half-dozen of us were assigned to teach Religious Studies 1, the foundational introductory course in religion at the university. The course syllabus was largely designed by the chairman of the department and included readings as diverse as Samuel Beckett's *Waiting for Godot* and Huston Smith's *The Religions of Man*.

How exciting it was. The opportunity to teach the very materials we were learning, needless to say, significantly reinforced my learning process.

II—Leaving Home (1963–1974)

Toward the end of that first semester, however, in response to feedback we were receiving from our students, a group of us TAs began imagining the possibility of creating our own syllabi for the course. Why was it necessary for all of us to teach from the same course outline? We agreed, prior to a meeting with our faculty advisor and Phillips, the department chair, to lodge a protest. It was also agreed that I would articulate this proposal and that the rest of the group would support me.

The meeting took place in the mid-afternoon after all of our teaching was finished for the day. When the allotted time arrived, I stood up and announced our plan. Phillips listened carefully. When I was finished, looking steadily at me alone, he said, "Mr. Kramer—you will continue to teach Religious Studies 1 exactly as you are told. If you don't like it that way, you can leave the program!" For a brief moment, I waited. I waited to hear if any of my colleagues would support me as they had agreed. No one spoke. I sat down and said nothing more.

Phillips also encouraged me, more than any other professor, to visit India. When I returned, he asked me about my experiences. I said, "I saw God."

I was thinking of the time I was sitting at a resort lake in Nanital. At one moment, as I looked around at all the families lounging, playing, and swimming in the lake, I was given to see their human expression of divinity.

Upon telling him about this, without seeming too pleased, Phillips said, "That's your ego speaking."

I immediately discounted his remarks, accurate though I now realize they were. Unfortunately, this was to be his final lesson and teaching for me. A year later, he would choke to death on several vitamin pills. It has taken me years to recognize the truth of his remark, and in the process to recognize that the true guru I had met in India was my own loneliness.

DeMartino's "True Self is Awakening Awakening to Itself"

He took notes on his own lectures.

He said he only answered questions on Zen if the questioner was ready and able to discuss the answer.

He kept the cold water dripping in his kitchen sink to remind him of the rock gardens in Kyoto's Buddhist monasteries.

He wore the same blue suit to every class, often removing its jacket.

He attracted notable performers to his classes (like Janice Ian) by word of mouth.

He rejected everything he wrote as soon as he finished/published it, and thus rarely published anything.

Years after I graduated, he allowed me to publish a dialogue with him, "Two Views of Self-Emptying: A Zen-Catholic Dialogue" (in *The Eastern Buddhist*, only after he meticulously edited every word he wrote and encouraged me to do the same).

In a graduate religious studies seminar, DeMartino once asked the class whether a light projected onto a screen symbolized the absolutely contradictory teachings of Zen.

Students who studied Buddha's True Self awakening answered affirmatively. Without speaking, DeMartino then projected a picture of an *enso* onto the screen, an empty, asymmetrical, spontaneously ink-brushed circle. "This is the emptiness or formless-form of the True Self," he said. "There is no formlessness without form."

I heard it, but my dualistically conditioned Baptist mind didn't "get it."

Though I went to graduate school to study the then-new interdisciplinary field of religion and literature, eventually completing a dissertation on T.S. Eliot's *Four Quartets*, it was Zen's logic-busting *koans* and knee-buckling teachings that riveted me.

II—Leaving Home (1963–1974)

What profoundly drew me away from my Baptist roots, what revised everything I had learned and practiced until then, was Buddhism, especially "Zen Awakening," especially Rinzai Zen "Nothingness," especially the Kyoto School's "Formless Form," especially as taught by Shin'ichi Hisamatsu through Richard DeMartino. Zen sought me and would not let go. Taught by D.T. Suzuki and Hisamatsu in Japan, DeMartino's Zen continually challenged me with questions that I couldn't answer. I tried, but I simply tangled myself in spiritual knots. I identified strongly, however, with what DeMartino called: "Awakening awakening to itself," not that I understood it at first!

His method included five cardinal principals: 1) *initial nature*, or the condition of human existence as the underlying problem; 2) *the fundamental*, or *root, problem* of human existence; 3) *the solution*, or nature of the most thorough-going resolution to that problem; 4) *the methodology*, or method-less ways to bring about that resolution; and 5) *the result*, or the "then what?" question. According to DeMartino, all of the world's great religions can be analyzed through this analytical structure. For years, I used his methodology.

Girls, it's important for me to pass on these slivers of teaching that have deeply captured me. To this day, I've saved DeMartino's dissertation, which I think brilliantly presents the intellectual purity of Kyoto Rinzai Zen Buddhism. DeMartino, of course, would have disagreed with me.

I hope it gets saved. Somebody, someday, somewhere will want to read its utterly unique perspective on Zen.

Friedman's "All Real Living is Dialogic Encounter"

In the late summer of 1968, Temple's Religion Department's PhD program was relatively new. Its faculty was full of creative energy and the students who came in the late '60s were full of a willingness to stretch, to grow, and to overcome previous limitations. Because it is so unusual to look at a single educational event from two sides (from the student's perspective and the professor's), I begin with an event that occurred long after I first met Professor Friedman.

After retiring from teaching in 1992 (at age seventy), Friedman presented four days of lectures and discussions at the Indira Gandhi National Centre for the Arts. He told me later that he presented his material, which became a book, *Intercultural Dialogue and the Human Image*, without a single note or the use of a single text. In it, Friedman said:

> One of the very best graduate students I ever had told me that students in the English department (this was also at Temple University) told him he should write his doctoral dissertation on some obscure person because it had not been done. I told him, "You ought not to do that. You ought to do something that is really meaningful to you." And he did. He wrote a brilliant dissertation on T.S. Eliot's *Four Quartets*.

It was through the "Religion and Literature" program that he founded and directed at Temple, but also through the impact of his book *To Deny Our Nothingness*, that I first came to meet Maurice. My earliest significant memory of him was learning in his seminars to avoid the temptation to reduce literature to "contents," or "themes," or "symbols" and to develop a dialogical approach to religion and human experience instead.

"I have always felt," I recall Friedman saying in one of his graduate seminars, "that the two central statements in Buber's *I and Thou* were, first,

II—Leaving Home (1963–1974)

'all real living is meeting,' and second, what Buber says of the I-Thou relationship: 'by the graciousness of its comings and the solemn sadness of its goings, it teaches you to meet others and to hold your ground when you meet them.'"

And then, switching his mood, he said, "It's not easy of course, not at all when the ground itself shifts." He laughed and then proceeded to tell us the story behind his laughter; it generated more, this time richer, more playful laughter. And that, I would discover, was how he conducted his classes with a rich blend of the most serious existentialist thoughts intermixed with laughter-provoking remarks.

One of the most indelible memories that remains with me from Friedman's seminars was the way he illustrated the movement between two-sided "I-Thou" relationships and objectifying "I-It" relations. "Buber distinguishes between an I-Thou knowing and an I-It knowledge," Friedman explained, "the I-It knowledge comes again and again from the I-Thou knowing. It is not, as we imagine, some objective reality in itself. Rather, it is a swinging back and forth between I-It and I-Thou."

Extending his right hand, he would then trace an invisible infinity sign with his hand, his fingers turning upside-down as they delicately traced their way back up the curve and then turning facedown upon reaching the top of the other curve.

By focusing on the central significance of Buber's dialogical philosophy, Friedman encouraged me to engage with literature in ways that addressed me personally and that, again and again, drew me into dialogue with a speaking text. But how powerfully life-changing Buber's words, along with Friedman's clarifications and applications.

But what makes dialogue genuine? Could there be anything more liberating? What makes dialogue genuine, according to Friedman, is found in neither one, nor the other of the partners, nor in both together, but in their interchange—in the Between.

I am so glad you girls would come to meet Maury—to swim and play ping pong at his San Diego Pool. As you remember, right up through all his writing projects, we worked together, especially on *Dialogically Speaking: The Interdisciplinary Thought of Maurice Friedman* that I would edit, and his last Buber book, *My Friendship with Martin Buber* that I would help him to publish.

It was a great honor to be able to be part of his life's-end-work, especially his final book about Martin Buber.

Fidelity to the Task

My Faithful Daughters,

Have you girls ever had a close friend who was so brilliant, so inspirational, and so talented that you were awed? One who encouraged your growth and challenged you to your core?

There was a fourth teacher, Dan Shea, who deeply influenced me at Temple. When I befriended this thin, 6'4" Irish student, a philosopher who wrote poetry, let his hair grow long, and wore an old cowboy hat, we discussed everything from books to films, from teachers to musicians.

One sunny day after lunch in 1971, in my graduate apartment, I asked Dan, "I've indicated to you several things I really admire about you. And yet you've never identified any of my character traits you really admire. What might one of them be?"

He looked up at me with a smirk and said, "Fidelity to the task. You complete what you begin."

You know how you are drawn to some people upon first meeting them? When I first heard Dan introduce himself, sitting in a circle in Friedman's

II—Leaving Home (1963–1974)

"Religion and Literature" class, I was immediately taken into the unfolding journey of his unlikely personal roadmap. Not that he had been anywhere special, but the transparency of his internal journey was completely unlike anything I had ever seen.

Here was a challenge to the road I was on. Here was a person who didn't need to hear himself speak. Here was a linguistic magician speaking, on our first meeting, as if he already understood the meaning of what we were about to be taught. For the next three years, I stayed closest to Dan.

I still remember what he said in one of our seminars in response to a student asking the question: "How can these magnificent ideas that you are teaching us make a difference in our actual lives?"

Dan replied, "Each new idea becomes a stepping stone that forms a path before us on which we walk in the direction that we were heading."

In our many conversations, Dan provided me with memorable insights into the educational process. A gangly and not always a precise man, Dan led with his words. His eyes had a glint about them that wasn't to be denied. As I had, Dan came to Temple to study with Maurice Friedman in particular. But, as it turned out, Dan and I fell into the Zen pond and splashed around in it together while working on our PhDs.

One evening, when I walked into Friedman's seminar on Buber, he had spread our marked papers out on his desk for us to pick up on our way in. There, next to mine, was Dan's, titled: "On Not Swallowing It Whole."

Though I've never read it, I've never forgotten the significance of the title. Unteachingly, Dan taught me not to swallow any teaching whole, to see through the veneer, the skin, and to encounter a deeper center there.

Meanwhile, I went on to finish my dissertation on T.S. Eliot's *Four Quartets*. Dan never submitted a dissertation. When his committee rejected his proposal for a dissertation on his own poetry, Dan left academia. He simply deserted a sinking ship, but not without taking me on an LSD journey with him.

It was the fall of 1971. I had just completed my PhD at Temple. I was with Dan, who had agreed to be my guide. It was to be my first acid trip. The most intense thing I had done prior to that was smoking marijuana—hardly in the same league. Yes, girls, I was once young and experimental, too.

Dan took me to his friend's farm just outside of the outskirts of Philadelphia. We each began by ritually ingesting the psychoactive tablet and then sitting back. While Dan was inside talking to a friend, I wandered outside to play with his friend's four-year old daughter in her sandbox. Feeling extremely comfortable inside my skin, it was as if I had never seen a grain of sand before. Each grain seemed to become clearly what it really was, almost as if my eyes had increased their magnification.

What I didn't realize was that my tripping consciousness had overcome/replaced my ordinary consciousness. I was completely content to continue playing with the little girl, when I suddenly heard Dan's voice "Ken, don't get stuck in the sandbox."

What he said then has stayed with me since. Both religious and academic traditions can be viewed as sandboxes. They can free your intellectual imagination to play with ideas, but they can also trap you and leave you with no foundation upon which to stand.

Baptist to Buddhist

My Ever-Seeking Girls,

Okay, I was a conservative Baptist. But what does that mean? Conservative North American Baptists are shut-down: no dancing, no extra marital sex, no gambling, no drugs or alcohol, a literal interpretation of scripture, and attending Church regularly. Traditionally, they also harbor negative attitudes towards "the Jews," which, of course, totally overlooks the fact that Jesus was a Jew (something I don't ever remember hearing said in Church). We were taught, instead, to pray for the Jews who, as non-believers, were doomed to Hell.

> "Jesus loves me.
> This I know.
> For the Bible
> Tells me so."

We sang these words with great energy, great joy in Sunday School class. My teacher, Miss Clare—my first crush—was a combination of looks and holiness. I mention this because one afternoon, a wave of infatuation swept over me. With no ability to resist, I spontaneously kissed her on the back of her hand. Then, just as quickly, I ran from the room. When I told my mother, who was waiting for me, what I had done, shaking with embarrassment, she didn't scold me as I thought she might. Instead, she insisted only that I go back and apologize to Miss Clare. This I did with a feeling of relief that, somehow, apologizing made the kiss legitimate.

What finally drew me away from my Baptist roots, what revised everything I had learned and practiced until then, was Buddhism, especially Rinzai's "Zen Awakening," and Hisamatsu's "Formless Form," which continually challenged me with questions I couldn't answer. Friedman's

Buberian perspective seemed, in contrast to Zen, like just another position in western philosophy that a student could elect to learn.

I chose Zen's radical, non-dualistic answer over Buber's dialogical openness to questions because nothing else I ever encountered in theological school called me deeper into self-examination, or convinced me more thoroughly that my Baptist faith, which now appeared intellectually simplistic, was not a place I wanted to stand. Certain elements of it even began to embarrass me.

The Materializing Guru

Namaste, Sweethearts!

In the early seventies when I undertook two adventures, I did not yet know that I had to travel East before I could return to the West—"as if," in the words of T.S. Eliot, "for the first time." I knew where I was going in the summer of 1972, though, and why. I purchased a round-trip ticket to India to visit gurus and Ashrams and to live with the people as much as possible.

I began by visiting Neem Karoli Baba's ashram in Nanital, north of New Delhi. Several Westerners were sitting around in a dorm room waiting for the Maharaji's return when I turned to a young man with a freshly-growing beard and wire-rimmed glasses who looked around my age. "What brought you to India?" I asked.

Without blinking an eye, he replied, "The square root of negative one."

"Why that?" I asked, bewildered and curious.

He smiled. "I am a mathematician. The one thing in mathematics that has always puzzled me is the symbol for an imaginary number. That's what the square root of negative one is. I came here to understand the fuller meaning of imaginary numbers."

I knew immediately that this mathematician had a better grasp of why he was here than I did.

I always thought that if I was going to describe what occurred over the next few months as I traveled around India in sandals, pajama pants, and a long, flowing shirt (to match my long flowing hair), I would write about the different gurus I met: Shiva Bali Yoga, or The Mother, or Neem Karoli Baba, or Ramsuratkumar, or Sathya Sai Baba.

The Materializing Guru

But what impressed me most about India was its music. Before then, I had been listening to a wide range of late '60s and early '70s rock, especially Crosby, Stills, Nash, and Young, Cat Stevens, rock operas (from The Who, to Procol Harum, and The Moody Blues), Bob Dylan, and The Beatles. The music in India, on the other hand, was altogether different, mostly was twangy and high-pitched.

A month of these screeching sounds brought me to the Ganges River in Rishikish to a room that opened onto a mango orchard. The next morning, after taking a tab of LSD, I set off on a hike along the Ganges seeking to find the Beatles' guru. No luck. I did meet and communicate with a holy man living in a tent. Remarkably enough, for at least an hour, we were able (with him speaking Hindi and me speaking English) to communicate with each other as if we each understood what the other was saying. Given the

II—Leaving Home (1963–1974)

potency of the LSD and the potency of his spirituality, I continued on my journey without questioning this mystery.

Upon returning to the mango orchard that evening, I was greeted by loud Western music emanating from a large black boom box. Two young Americans had moved in next to me. Under a full moon, still under the influence of acid in the Indian environment, I hear The Rolling Stones singing "You can't always get what you want." More accurately, I hear the English Boy's Choir singing it in the mango garden under a full moon:

> You can't always get what you want
>
> But if you try sometimes
>
> You just might find
>
> You get what you need

"There it is!" I exclaimed to myself. "That's the real mantra I will take with me back to America."

Yet the most memorable event occurred when I wandered along a dirt road outside the diminutive village of Puttaparthi, where thousands had gathered to celebrate the festival of Guru Poornima—the full moon in July—by visiting Sai Baba, the guru with an afro who produced miracles.

After five days in the vicinity of the ashram, I was disappointed. I had not yet seen Baba's materializations up close. So I decided to leave the next day, a day before the festival ended, to avoid the rush.

That evening, I took my place with the men (the women sat to the left side of the ashram entrance). As usual, when Sai Baba, the materializing guru, appeared, he walked first amid the ranks of women devotees, now and again, stretching his arm out to hand over something I couldn't see. After a while, he walked toward where I was sitting and began speaking in Tamil to a man and his sons sitting beside me.

This was as close as I had ever come to him, or to any guru (I didn't dare take his picture. *How do you take a picture of God*? I thought). He wore a long saffron robe, which accentuated his amazingly bushy hair, which devotees said was caused by the electrical currents constantly passing through his body. He had kindness in his eyes and a small crinkle on his nose. He walked with grace and a serene smile.

Suddenly, he turned to me and said in clear English: "So you're leaving tomorrow, are you!" His tone was declarative, not questioning. In that same instant, he extended his arm. As he turned his palm upward from a facedown position, I saw the Vibuthi (the ash of cow dung that has been

The Materializing Guru

blessed by the guru) materialize in his outstretched hand. It wasn't there, and then it was.

"Take it; eat it!" he said. I was told three times, and the man sitting next to me poked me in the ribs after the second time. I hadn't heard because I was no longer in my body. His poking returned me to body-consciousness.

Without hesitation, I took the perfumed sacramental ash of cow dung and ate it. "It's a cure for whatever is wrong with you," a devotee later said to me. "It's associated with Shiva," another said. "It means we all return to dust."

After Sai Baba returned to the ashram and his devotees began dispersing, I climbed to my rooftop accommodations, swimming in the reverberation of what had just occurred.

But what *had* just occurred?

Wide-awake, I lay on the flat roof on my back, and gazed up at the evening sky. To the east, the full moon was rising, too big to be real, too bright to be believed. To the west, the full sun was setting. I felt extremely comfortable.

But what really happened? Everything occurred exactly as I described. Yet, that in it of itself, seemed beyond the bounds of credibility. I only know that what I experienced exists in my consciousness in the form of a dream-like memory.

In the end, it was just a stage, and an early one at that. I was chasing after personal awakening as if, in finding it, I would find not only what most people at that time were searching for, but also what I thought was most needed for the spiritual evolution of my own consciousness.

Just imagine, girls, the audacity that fueled my search, and the state of my under-developed soul at the time!

Loneliness

My Lovely Yvonne and Leila,

I was lonely.

When I was thirty, I was something of a spiritual romantic (no, much more than something of one), which is why I took off for Mother India searching for the heart of awareness. Before I departed, an acquaintance of mine who sold used books in Mt. Airy said that I would probably, in his words, "come back in a box."

While I didn't come back unchanged, I didn't come back in a box, either (or did I?). I never saw that acquaintance again to ask what the hell he meant by his ominous prediction, but I wish I had.

I was lonely partly because I was in an awkward marriage with Joanne. By the spring of 1972, we were in the fourth year of our uneventful marriage. I say "uneventful" because we were far too normal to satisfy the abnormality streaking through my being. Perhaps she felt that way, too. I remember once that she flipped out and shut down for a day and a half: she didn't want anything to eat, didn't want to do anything, didn't know who she was, and didn't seem to care. This freakish turn of events however, neither lasted long nor ever returned. Otherwise, we were "normal."

I was absurdly self-conscious and my number one priority throughout the marriage was whatever writing project I was working on at the time. I was both arrogantly naïve and eager to please, a combination that continued/s to trip me up.

Think about it: on the one hand, I was worldly immature, on the other, highly intellectual; I was sexually innocent yet rhetorically appealing. Make of it what you can—it led us down the path of separation which first began when Joanne and I agreed that while I sauntered forth to India for the summer, she would take a road trip in our VW Bus to California and then we'd meet back in Philly at the summer's end.

Loneliness

Incomprehensible language and unbearable Indian heat greeted my aloneness with so much discomfort that I almost got back on a plane and returned to Philadelphia the very next day after my arrival! It was only by eating large quantities of watermelon that I could survive the cockroach infested, bloodstained sheets in the room where I spent my first night. I was travelling by myself. I knew no one, and it took every act of courage I could muster to not return home (as many others had before me).

One of my motives for travelling to India that summer was to find some peace in being separated from Joanne. But while it didn't take long for me to separate myself from my Western garb (jeans/shirt) and exchange them for pajama pants and long-sleeved, loose fitting shirts, loneliness was another deal.

Accompanied with the realization that marriage sometimes widens rather than fills the already-existing cracks in the relationship, loneliness was having its way with me.

Girls, imagine you're in India, land of a hundred thousand awakenings, seeking nothing less than your own personal vision. Imagine sitting in a ten-day workshop guided by Goenka, a well-known Buddhist meditation teacher. Imagine the simple instruction to count your each inhalation and each exhalation in order to focus on the rhythm of your breathing. Simple, right? Not for me. I couldn't get the image of Joanne out of my mind.

The dry heat intensified being all alone (no computers, no smartphones, no gadgets). I sent "Dear Joanne" postcards from everywhere but with no return address. That . . . was me. I had become a man with no return address who didn't know where he was going or how he would get there. I only knew I would return at summer's end.

My mind insisted, *insisted* on continuing to fill itself with thoughts and memories of her, which is painfully apparent to me now reading back through the journal I kept while in India.

> May 28th, 1972
>
> Before leaving, speaking with Joanne about the necessity of splitting this summer (of us making separate trips alone and finding independence independently.) . . .
>
> June 4th, 1972
>
> Joanne, your face is alive in my mind, a picture of love and its tragic gesture. I am distraught; I am lonely.

II—Leaving Home (1963–1974)

June 5th, 1972

Arriving and immediately wanting to return, immediately home and never to complain again about Philadelphia water.

June 12th, 1972

On a train ride, Joanne: "how much I want to speak with you, long to have you here . . ." I cry for you, Joanne. I cry for myself without you. I am alone, Joanne. Why did I come here?

July 13th, 1972

(Calcutta evening): Feeling down on India again. Downpour! Soaked! Joanne: from the cauldron of hell all passages to you are blocked, my mind is a prison; feelings a weapon, again this self.

July 20th, 1972

(Aurobindo): The return of vision again which calls into words first feelings for you—and you are only here, no matter where else, the reason for my not being able to be away from your presence—no matter where you are.

August 2nd, 1972

(Aurangabad): Beyond this world is another quite unique, and we have the chance to discover the pain of our pasts which was good enough to drive us apart but bad enough to get us that way in the first place. You are the center of my deepest concentration—my life to your life—a yoga in a new language.

August 5th, 1972

I cannot concentrate; my mind speeds ahead to the future with you, Joanne, so much that I feel it is time to leave India, to be with you again, even if you are not at home. I'll join you wherever you are . . . Joanne help me. I pray to your heart, which I know is as pure as energy.

Loneliness

I was alone, without a friend, without an English-speaking acquaintance, without a vehicle, without knowing what to do in the next moment.

I have, before now, always tried to keep these deep feelings that accompanied me through my travels hidden. I've covered them up with stories of my experiences with gurus, with my best cleverness.

It turned out that loneliness, as I would much later realize, was my true guru.

The Forbidden Kiss

Devoted Daughters,

I returned from India with a fully grown beard, long hair, fantastic guru stories, several chillum pipes for smoking marijuana, and a detailed green, cloth-covered diary filled with impassioned outpourings to Joanne: "I can't wait to see you again!" and "Forgive me for being so selfish when I was with you!" and "I am fully ready to begin our marriage again!" Of course, she wasn't home. She was in California, and she wanted me to fly there so that we could drive our VW Bus back to Philly.

How wonderful it was to see my blonde-haired, tanned tank-topped beautiful lady. Oh, that first kiss at the San Francisco airport! All my juices were flowing.

It felt wonderful being together again, even though I was jealous when I heard of the few men that she had met in the meantime. I only met gurus! She met good-looking young men! I was trying to separate the world of the flesh from the world of the spirit. She, on the other hand, lived in just one world and probably wasn't thinking of me as much as I was of her.

But back we drove. We made love each evening until we were in the middle of Montana, where our car stalled at a little gas station whose mechanic promised to fix it as soon as the needed part arrived in a few days. Fortunately, behind the little gas station was a little motel, no doubt, for just such occasions.

There we were, with nothing to do. Just us two. Wait a minute, what about my not being able to wait until I saw her again? What about the "Ain't no doubt about it, you're just what I need" spirit? It was dissolving in front of me, and we weren't even back to the comforts of our home yet.

I tell these things to you girls to better situate my behavior that following Thanksgiving. Joanne had prepared a magnificent meal to which she invited some friends, along with a European looking brunette woman

The Forbidden Kiss

whom, Joanne said, had been dating Cat Stevens, who, unfortunately, had just dumped her. The meal began. Each of us was enjoying our food then, no!! Cat Stevens' voice suddenly was heard emanating from the radio playing in the background.

"Morning has broken,

like the first morning..."

Joanne's friend immediately began crying, and ran upstairs.

I had been admiring the well-proportioned, stylishly dressed girl throughout the meal every chance I could. Since no one seemed to know what to do next, I gallantly volunteered to see if I could offer any solace. I walked upstairs. She was sitting on the edge of our king-sized bed, her face buried in her hands, still crying.

She looked despondently beautiful. "Is there anything I can do?" I stupidly stammered, knowing exactly what I would like to do.

Her short black dress was pulled high by her crossed legs. When she didn't answer my question, I slowly walked toward her and sat on the bed next to her. She was wiping tears from her eyes. Nervously, I leaned over and placed my right hand softly on her shoulder. I was fearful all the while that she might feel affronted.

Instead, she quickly looked up, smiled, and leaned toward me. As she came closer, I almost threw my eyes into her body. I don't know who was more surprised—she, that I was her friend's husband; or me, that I was sitting this closely to my wife's friend on our bed.

Now what?

What was I thinking? Was I thinking? No, I was not. Here was a beautiful, sad-eyed young woman who desperately needed to be consoled. And I could definitely offer consolation. I began rubbing her shoulder. She leaned into my chest. She felt so soft. The already narrow distance between us seemed to dissolve into a newly familiar connection. I felt like locking the door and throwing away the key. All of my resistance was growing helpless.

I kissed her willing lips first softly, then deeply. She reached up and pulled me into her breasts. In the next nanosecond, just before falling back onto the bed, we stopped.

We stopped as suddenly as we had begun, without a word. We found ourselves between here and lost. A light went out. Would I ever know where I belonged? We did know that we shouldn't go any further—indeed, had already gone too far. We pulled back from our embrace. "We should go

II—Leaving Home (1963-1974)

downstairs..." I said. She agreed almost as if nothing had happened, and we rejoined Joanne at the dining room table.

After we finished the meal, I excused myself so they could talk. Later that evening, after Joanne's friend had left, I knew our marriage was over. My indiscretion had ended it.

I was not able to lie to Joanne. When she asked me what had happened, I gave her an apology-laced accounting. Of course, I didn't repeat—I couldn't repeat—how luscious the forbidden kiss had tasted and how exciting it still was.

My "I am really, really sorry," sounded hollow to me. I'm sure the same was true for her. It was clear to each of us that our summer of separation and fall of reconciliation had now died on the vine. From this point forward, Joanne planned and then executed her departure. It was mutually agreed that she would take half the value of everything we had, including the value of our house. We initiated divorce papers. Four years of marriage—finished.

I was distraught. Joanne and I had been a good couple; we had shared many wonderful times together. She was my first everything. The first few days after it was over and she left, I was broken down. I felt like a failure. Felt desolate and useless. Damn my Baptist conscience!

What I had done was wrong. If Joanne had done it, I would have been outraged. Clearly, I was not fit to be her (or anyone's?) husband. It could be said, I suppose, that I had given her a gift. My misdeed gave her every reason to leave me, as she should have. I had cheated. So much for my moral compass. So much for the right of my fidelity. So much for responsible trustworthiness.

On an erotic whim, I had disassembled our entire marriage. My lips were complicit. I never again saw the girl whose name I have long ago forgotten. And after Joanne left for California, I saw her once, and then never again.

Neither of us has ever tried to contact the other. I tried to make my heart a home for Joanne. I lied. I swore I'd be true. But again, I lied.

Off she went, and I went back to teaching at LaSalle.

The Gypsy Lady

My Incredible Gifts,

If I still can't believe it, how could I expect anyone else to? But this is how it happened. This is how "we" got started:

Even before my divorce with Joanne (who was by then back in California) was finalized, I met and then, on my third day of knowing her, moved your soon-to-be-mother, Gaelyn, into my Mt. Airy home. It started with a tightly fitting charcoal sequined blouse that boldly announced the brilliance of her hourglass figure.

My good friend, Aaron Levine, and I (each living wife-lessly in a Quincy street house) had just finished broadcasting our one-hour experimental FM radio broadcast, "Mixed Media Workshop," in Center City Philadelphia. Aaron would grab a stack of vinyl and I, a stack of books. Without rehearsal, he played music and when it seemed appropriate, I would read a paragraph from a philosopher, or a mystic, a poet or a children's story, on top of the music. Endless fun was ours, with no accountability.

After our show one evening, Aaron and I went to a night club/restaurant filled with young hipsters. I can still see her beautiful figure waiting on other tables and I immediately asked her if she could wait on ours. Picture this: I'm sitting, she's standing; I'm sneaking eye-level glances of her breasts. Come on—those breasts and her gypsy-clad body—whoa! She, on the other hand, was captivated by what I was saying. And what was I saying?

"When are you finished with work tonight?" I asked, blinking up at her.

"At midnight," she responds, with an unreserved openness, her hand on her hip, knowing exactly what my next question will be.

"Can I pick you up when you're done working?"

"Yes," she said, her smile beaming down at me.

II—Leaving Home (1963-1974)

That "yes" set me flying. *So what* that was I normally in bed by 11:30? So what that it was at least a half hour drive (sometimes longer) from my Mount Airy house to the center city club where she worked? She said "Yes!"

That "yes" also contained a yes to many questions: Would I ever be accepted by such a beauty? Could I possibly walk into a trendy Philadelphia nightspot and walk out with a new future? Why did I have the courage on this particular evening to approach this particular girl at this particular moment in time? And would she sleep with me?

The fact that she was a drop dead brunette beauty with *that* body had completely overcome, overwhelmed, and undone me. I apologize if it is weird for you girls to hear me talk this way. But hold on tight . . .

So, home I went, unable to stop thinking about her. It was three hours until I could go back, and there were no distractions strong enough to ease my racing thoughts. Luckily, Aaron, who had been at the café with me and who had met her as well, agreed to sit at the kitchen table with me while we talked about nothing else but her.

At midnight exactly, I walked into the trendy south Philadelphia club. She was ready. She was smiling. I was moving without moving and yet instinctively following her lead. When we arrived at my house, we sat on the living room rug in front of a fire and fell so deeply, so boundary-breakingly into timeless conversation that the plan-for-sex never began, even though there were pauses in the conversation for marijuana-enhanced passionate kisses. Immediately, all of everything was Gaelyn.

There was no hurry. In my mind, she wasn't going anywhere. But suddenly, at 4:30am, she said she would have to leave to attend an early morning psych class.

And then, the second night, after waiting all day with Aaron and not knowing what to do with myself other than to tell him how remarkably, incredibly, amazingly over-the-top she had been the night before and how I was hopelessly falling head-over-heels for her without even knowing anything other than that I needed to find out in order to be as close as possible to every inch of her, to every aspect of her, to every contour of her magnificent grace as was possible. When I went to her apartment that second night, she said she was unable to leave with me but that she would see me next day. Only later did I find out that there was another man in her apartment that evening.

And then, on the third day, picking her up at school, taking her back to her apartment, getting naked in the bathtub with her, helping her gather up some clothes, taking her to my house, and carrying her across the threshold with the remark "We're married."

There were times when we only made it halfway up the stairs before stopping for sex. There were times when she introduced me to places, and positions, and techniques that I had never even fantasized about, let alone done. You get the picture; this was one innocent thirty-year-old dude being exposed to one experienced twenty-year-old sexy lady.

But Gaelyn brought many other new things into my life, as well—a hip style (especially in clothing) and taste (especially in entertainment, and an interest in the arts) like the live Dylan concert we saw from the third row (we actually arrived an hour late, having forgotten to set our clocks ahead for daylight savings time, so it was a good thing there was an opening band). Imagine seeing and hearing Dylan up close!

How many times . . .

Like a rolling stone . . .

The times, they are a-changin' . . . .

But it was the smaller venues that she introduced me to where we heard Robbie Robertson and The Band, who sometimes backed up Bob Dylan and Bonnie Raitt, the latter of whom I had never heard before. Oh my—what I had been missing!

Then there was Hall & Oats, one of whom she knew personally. Ah . . . jealousy: how many faces it assumed; how quickly it strikes.

But the biggest introduction was to the Canadian singer Joni Mitchell, to her album *Blue* and to songs like: "All I Want," "River," and "A Case of You." With her guitar or piano accompanying her, her story-full lyrics dug deeply into my emotions.

But by far, the greatest gifts that Gaelyn brought into our relationship were you beautiful girls.

Leila Ann

My Shining Daughter,

Leila—brilliant lady—never could I have suspected that you would become *you*! From your eyes barely focusing, to a vibrant, vivacious "hard-headed woman." No fancy dancer who moves so smoothly but has no answers.

You realize, of course, that the unknowable, unnamable, invisable One resides in your name, reminding you that She/He shines in/through/around your each breathing moment. It was during my summer in India that the Sanskrit term for the Ever Present Holy One—Lila (the play/dance of God)—caught my attention.

I tell you this to provide a context for what happened when you were born a year later.

What a perfect early November day—crisp, blue-skied, welcoming—a new life. We were standing before Duchamp's "Bicycle Wheel" at the Philadelphia Art Museum when Gaelyn said excitedly, "Ken . . . Ken! My water just broke." Fortunately, the Birthing Center was not far from the art museum, and off we drove in our green Dodge van.

Then, you. You opened your eyes. New birth! New life! New you!

New parents, too . . . reaching out, holding you, feeding you, and singing to you.

There you were, wrapped in a blanket, living, breathing, squirming, and crying, your head against mother's milk-filled breasts. Our baby—nothing else mattered.

Just before Gaelyn was about to take her first shower, we were suddenly confronted with an administrator from the Birthing Center asking the $500 question, "What do you want to name your daughter?"

We had decided to take our new baby home to live with her first, to get to know her, and to let her "name herself."

But life is bigger than we are. We didn't get our way and, in not getting our way, we did. The administrator's response was, "Okay, then her name will appear on the birth certificate as Baby Girl Kramer. Then, when you decide on her name, it will cost you $500 to change it."

Neither of us wanted to spend $500. We each said, "Give us a bit more time to think about this."

What happens next is epic.

Gaelyn says, "While I take a shower, listen to the sounds she makes when she cries. It's all we've got," and off she went to the shower. It turned out to be an inspired suggestion.

Red-faced and crying, you filled the silence with "A's" and "L's" which together sounded like "Allah."

"You want to be named for God," I realized, "Alright, but not Allah." Then what?

Before I had time to deliberate, the Sanskrit name "Lila" struck a chord in me. Perfect. When Gaelyn returned from her shower, an objective observer would not have been able to detect a difference between our energies. Each of us was excited with totally encompassing joy.

"How about Lila for a name!" I exclaimed.

"Ken, you are not going to believe this," she replied. "I forgot to tell you that at the moment she was delivered, Sai Baba materialized and reached into my womb to pull the baby's head out."

"What?!"

"And that's not all. When I was in the shower, sort of day-dreaming, letting the water cascade over my body, I heard the name 'Leila' (the Hebrew spelling), but I thought you wouldn't like it so I decided not to tell you."

Not only did you name yourself, but we saved ourselves $500. You are remarkably blessed, an "old soul," as mother Jennie (a channeler) said when she first saw you.

Your middle name came easily to us. After we had agreed on "Leila," we looked for a middle name starting with "A." Gaelyn then suggested "Ann," the name of her best friend in high school, who was killed by a drunk driver.

"That way," she said, "following the Jewish tradition, Ann's memory will be carried on into the next generation by Leila Ann."

Take it in. Rejoice. Now the moment is all yours to share.

II—Leaving Home (1963–1974)

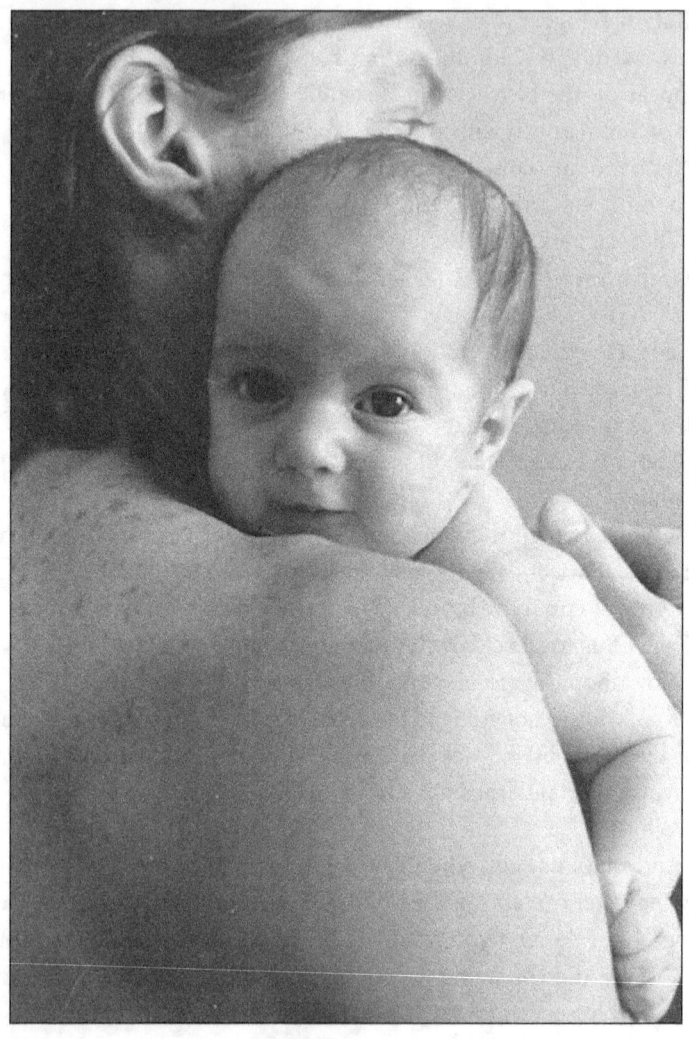

Not that it surprises me, but you couldn't have chosen a more real-life, appropriate name. Shine on, you dancer, you creator, you healer. Shine on.

III

Traveling West

(1974–2000)

Santa Cruz

Dearest Yvonne and Leila,

Early in the summer of 1974, Gaelyn and I left Mt. Airy in North Philadelphia with an eight-month old Leila, and headed west.

Why, you girls may wonder, after being born and raised in Philadelphia, did mom and I move cross-country to Santa Cruz?

Frank Rizzo, that's why.

Not solely, but when the infamous anti-youth Police Commissioner became Philadelphia's mayor at a time when we were reading Abby Hoffman's *Steal This Book*, it was easy to agree that we did not want to raise you in that atmosphere. And when Rizzo's response to the question, "How is the city going to handle the anticipated glut of cars coming to Philadelphia's 1976 bi-centennial celebration?" was, "Pave over Fairmount Park." No. We sang instead from Joni Mitchell's "The Big Yellow Taxi," in which she sings, "they paved paradise and put up a parking lot." It was definitely time to leave.

We left brimming with excitement in our used green-and-white Dodge van, which allowed us to place a playpen for you in the open space just behind us. Armed with dozens of tapes of late '60s and early '70s music, a pound of Indian hash, and half a dozen copies of *Mother Earth News*, we headed west with the visionary goal to locate paradise there.

III—Traveling West (1974–2000)

In advance of our western departure, I had sent off a letter to *Mother Earth News* describing our vision:

> We have these dreams in common: a love of the earth, running water and rock gardens, handcrafted poems, private space within an ecological community, gardening food and fruits, chickens and a goat or so and horses, dry and warm climate as in the Southwest United States, alternative education which is not just another face of the "banking theory," room for children and laughter and *high* times in the old barn whenever, and alternative sources of power if possible. We are looking for "a place" to buy or for others to join us or for others, already there, to welcome us. We do not feel we have to start actualizing our dream alone and would be quick to join in with those who have already begun, and whose energies and directions we could complement.
>
> Driving across the country, feeling invincible, with our love for you, Leila, how could we know what lay ahead?

Aside from locating some alternative community where we could live and grow our own food, I was also looking for a university town where

Santa Cruz

I might be able to find employment. Boulder, Colorado, therefore, was our first destination, both because of the University of Colorado and the Naropa Buddhist Institute, which was in its initial stages at the time. No luck was found at either place.

Two key memories of our time in Boulder have never left me. The first was a chance encounter we had in a "head shop." We had lost our hash pipe and needed to replace it. In the midst of the bright colors and Joni Mitchell sounds and burning incense and patchouli oil-scented bodies and laughter, we fell into a conversation with other travelers who inquired about our destination.

"We don't know," I said, glancing at Gaelyn and then back at the scruffy black-bearded store clerk. "We're looking for an alternative community somewhere where we can grow some of our own vegetables. But there also has to be a university connected with the town so that I might find employment." I shifted you, Leila, from my left shoulder to my right shoulder. You laid your head on me and looked around at all the bright and moving colors with wide eyes.

At that moment, a young man who had overheard what I had just said remarked, "You should look into Swanton, near Santa Cruz, California. It's a small community by the ocean with a fairly new university and a lot of people living alternative lifestyles. I've spent some time there and I think you would really enjoy it," he added. Having never heard of Santa Cruz, I didn't, at the time, give what he said much attention—I was more intent on finding the best marble pipe.

The second key memory happened that evening. As it turned out, one of the founders of the Naropa Institute, Chögyam Trungpa, author of a then-bestselling book *Cutting Through Spiritual Materialism*, was going to lecture on Buddhism in the downtown moving picture theater. This news excited me, first, because he was involved with the still-forming university and second because I had read his book and found it filled with nuggets of spiritual wisdom.

That evening, I showed up to a sold-out theater with my wide-eyed restlessness and my eight-month-old in my arms, and my wife by my side, having tasted the intoxicating herb, hashish, on the way. Nevertheless, with an audacity that was supported by the status-giving insights I had gained from my summer in India, bolstered by my PhD in comparative religious traditions, and nurtured by three years of teaching eastern religions at LaSalle College, we walked into the theater expecting to hear him speak.

III—Traveling West (1974–2000)

When we approached the entrance door, through which we could see every seat filled and hear the crowd's anticipatory excitement, a young, blonde-haired woman greeted us and asked about our intentions. "I see that this event is sold out," I said, "but since we have just arrived from Philadelphia, and since I am a professor of religious studies and since I am interested in possibly teaching at the Naropa Institute, I am hoping that you will let us in."

Shaking her head, she said, "No, I can't do that."

"But we would be willing to sit on the floor," I said, pleading my case further. "Look at us, we're all very thin. We don't take up much room, and I really need to hear what he's going to say."

Even as I was finishing those words, her demeanor was shifting from a welcoming grin to a disappointed sadness. Tears began to well up in the beautiful girl's eyes. Within an instant, she was sobbing as if she had just learned that her dear dog had died. "I can't let you in," she moaned. "I'm sorry, I can't!"

Surprised by her emotional outburst, I asked her, "Is something wrong?"

She then revealed something that which gave me a gift I have never forgotten. "The reason I'm crying," she said, "is because this is really hard for me. I hate to tell people that they can't do something. I hate to say no. And that's why I'm here. Rimpoche put me here especially because he knows how difficult it is for me to say no. He put me here to practice saying 'no' to people."

That was the theme of his talk, which I never heard. Apologizing to her for being so insistent, we gathered ourselves and left. That was the lesson I most needed at that moment. I needed to hear, "No!"

Then, on a brilliant early July midday, thinking that we were on our way to Oregon, we saw signs to Santa Cruz.

"Gaelyn," I say, "do you remember that guy in the Boulder head shop?"

"Which one?"

"The one who suggested that we visit Swanton near Santa Cruz."

"Oh yeah, why do you ask?" she says, shifting her loosely fitting blouse to feed you, Leila.

"Look!" I say, pointing at the sign. "Maybe it was meant to be."

We followed the signs on Highway 1 North to downtown Santa Cruz, found a parking place, and sat at an outdoor café on Pacific Avenue, across from the Cooper House. People were dancing to the music of marijuana-inspired street musicians. Festivity was everywhere, and the moving picture swept us up.

We immediately fell in love with the European ambiance—the outdoor cafés, the casual, "mellow" people, the nearby beaches, the inland redwoods, the clean streets, and the rolling parks. Santa Cruz: a resplendent small city of hills and flat lands interrupted by the San Lorenzo River, which flows from the northern redwood-lined hills into the bay. Leila, you were particularly taken by the colorful clowns running around Pacific Avenue, spreading their light-hearted vibes. This was all before we rode through UCSC's acres of redwoods opening onto their panoramic ocean views, the deer feeding in the meadows. Once we did that, we were really hooked.

I remember standing beneath an old-growth redwood tree on UCSC's campus. I tried to hug it but I couldn't encircle it with my arms. I looked straight up along its massive trunk until I was dizzy with a different connection to Mother Nature than I had ever been afforded before.

The musical phrase, "Open your eyes, look up to the skies/And see" began echoing through my consciousness.

It would only be later that I would discover how rare redwood trees are. They only exist in a few places in the world. The decision to relocate our home to this place was, in hindsight, as brash as my announcing to your mother, after knowing her for just three days, that we were already married.

Yvonne Rose

My Unbelievable Gift,

When we first saw your smile, we couldn't forget you for one moment. You put a spell on us: our adopted daughter.

Several things needed to happen for us before you could come into our lives.

After the extremely difficult experience Gaelyn had delivering Leila (an abruption), she didn't want to give birth again. We agreed that, thereafter, if we were to have another child, we would adopt. But how? Where?

Most important, of course, as I've told you many times, was that fateful day on Rodeo Gulch Road when Leila started chanting: "I want a sister! I want a sister!" So it was finalized: we were going to adopt a baby girl. We had no idea, though, how truly blessed we were about to be by a pure blessing.

A short while later, Gaelyn told me that she was going to San Francisco for a photoshoot. Upon returning she said excitedly: "Guess what, Ken. I was talking with the photographer about wanting to adopt a girl. He gave me the number of his friend (your Uncle Dave), who is caring for his sister's child (you!). The immediate problem is that Dave is being called to New York City for his job." The primary reason was, of course, that Kathrine, your biological mother, couldn't continue to take care of you because of mental health issues.

This all happened so quickly and almost out of the blue that it made me nervous and unsure. Could this really be happening so suddenly?

Within what felt like about a week, we all visited your grandparents, Fred and Betty Sarbach. There you were: a beautiful, blond-haired, green-eyed girl who immediately and thoroughly captured our hearts. All of my anxiety vanished. We knew then and there that you were ours, and I remain amazed that a little girl whom I'd never met before, who I hadn't yet even spoken a word to, could inspire such an immense connection of love . . . Yvonne, you captured my soul in that moment.

Your grandparents agreed to an initial yearlong foster care arrangement to see if Kathrine would (or would be able to) change her mind. Fortunately for us, she was not able to take you back and the Sarbachs agreed that we could and should adopt you: Yvonne Maria Kramer.

It was an open adoption. We wanted the Sarbachs to enter into our family as much as they wanted us to enter into theirs. They often visited us, and we them. Leila began calling Fred and Betty "grandpa and grandma." The same was true of your uncle and aunts.

With Fred and Betty's agreement, the first thing I did was to officially change your middle name to Rose, my mother's name.

That act, for me, implanted you even more deeply into the family than even I suspected. It was as if, by giving you my mother's name, you received along with it her spirit of unconditional love.

So, you became Yvonne Rose Kramer. And I became the father of two daughters—the Kramer Sisters.

III—Traveling West (1974–2000)

At first, you were very reserved with us. You wouldn't be hugged, so we had to be patient. With Leila, though, you were playing almost right away—two sisters sharing and fighting over toys as if you had been raised together from the start.

Our love for you was warm and deep. You always seemed, to me, a divine gift for which I felt unworthy. As I grew to know you more and more, playing with you, loving you, and forming a daddy-daughter bond, the more I began to feel biologically connected. It was obvious that you were meant to be with us.

A large picture window in front of my desk still opens out onto the yard where you and Leila used to play. Centered above the window is a rectangular wooden plaque with curved corners, which you made for me in junior high. It reads: DAD'S DEN. It has hung above the window since.

And here's the thing—each time I look up at it, I see reflected in its letters moments from our history together: your arriving in a pretty blue flower-printed dress and white shoes (I still can't imagine what switching families was like for you!); your early years with us (me chasing you around in games of "you're it!"); school days (me attending your volleyball games and speaking in your AP English class); then you at community college (with me attending more volley-ball games); and then at San Diego State University; then your successful career as a sales person (finding the ladder from retail marketing to apparel sales to key account sales rep.).

And when I look up, I see your killer smile, there as it was when I saw you this morning as you opened the Cyprus Street door after my care-giver, Terina had knocked twice and turned away.

"She's here," I exclaimed, pointing back to the door.

"My daughter is here!"

SJSU

My Intelligent Girls,

But how did I land at San Jose State University? Before leaving Philadelphia, I sent out a letter (using a pompous impersonation of e.e. cummings' writing style) to several universities near where I thought we might wind up living. I was enthralled with the cummings' poetry, even assigning his well-known Harvard lectures, *i: six nonlectures*, for one of my classes at LaSalle. One of these letters went to Benton White, the coordinator of religious studies at SJSU. It was an irretrievably pretentious letter, so I'll let it speak for itself:

6617 quincy st
phila pa 19119
15sept73

dear chairman:

this letter intends to STAND OUT as an introduction.

i realize that teaching positions are overly-supplied and overly-demanded, but because of the synergistic, interdisciplinary nature of my writing/and/teaching, i might specifically advantage your department.

my educational purpose is: to lift the mystification of not-knowing from the realm of religion; to interpret the mirrowing finger of its discourse; & to presence it as the 100 percent actualization of its phenomena. along these insights my 1st book — "since i've gone" — (now being considered for publication by harper&row, avon and mentor) offers a new technique for the study of religion which enters the reunification of philosophy&art to perceive the "genealogy of solidity" as the very of religious discourse.

teaching that, phenomenological method dives into and is born of the perennial multi/particular Logos of religion. my

III — Traveling West (1974–2000)

classes thereby avoid the divide-and-subjugate mentality which reduces religion to historic puzzlement over data otherwise to be deflated by the social sciences. this "interdisciplinary attitude" has the advantage of being new all the way back to its assumption: the doing of Being/itself is stimul/temporal with "if you see with innocent eyes, everything is divine" (federico fellini).

in three colleges, including LaSalle where i now teach, i have offered courses in:

World Religions

Religions of the East

Religious Attitudes in Modern Literature

Phenomenology of Religion

Religion and Man's Search for Self

Modern British and American Poetry

to complement this introduction, i have enclosed a resume and a current course announcement. i would be happy to speak further with you about this.

thoughtfully,

kenneth kramer, phd.

As a result of the letter, I secured an interview. In hindsight, I am astonished that Professor J. Benton White was able to read through the fearlessly wrought hyperbole into the sensitive intellect behind it. I arrived at the interview in sandals, with a beard, and with my sensuous wife and one-year-old daughter. Or, as Benton saw it from his perspective:

> Ken Kramer had just returned from a summer in India, had a successful teaching career at Temple as well, and was particularly interested in world religions. He had married a woman who was bright and beautiful at the same time, she had actually been an exotic dancer I believe . . . They both looked like "Flower Children."
> . . . After an hour with Ken it was obvious how bright he was and that he was better prepared to teach World Religions than anyone else I had seen . . . Ken was everything I was not, a free spirit, very bright but non-traditional, and I thought the kind of person who would do what he said he would.
>
> J.B. White

SJSU

Several years passed before SJSU opened its doors to me. My earliest classes were in off-campus sites, including twice in Soledad State Prison's maximum-security unit. From the men there, I learned the significance of the phrase "crap-detector." They taught me to eliminate "crap" from my teaching as much as I could.

Fortunately, my early classes at State were well attended and, soon, I was a candidate for a tenure-track position, which was ultimately given to Christian Jochim, primarily because he had published a book, *Chinese Religions*, in the Prentice Hall Series.

I was crushed. I didn't want to be a realtor with a PhD selling houses. I wanted to teach.

I sent a letter to Benton in which I offered to teach "Catholic Tradition," a course that I had taught before, for no remuneration. Next, another strange twist of fate unfolded. Several weeks later, I received a call from Benton, who had not otherwise responded to my offer.

"Ken, how would you like to teach full-time at San Jose State?" he asked.

"What?!" It was as if I had just been struck by a lightening bolt.

I was hoping for an answer to my proposal, not this offer.

"Professor Keady" (who taught classes in "Western Religions," and two sections each semester of "Death, Dying and Religion") "has decided to move to the administrative side of campus and become the assistant dean of student affairs. This leaves his courses wide open. You would simply take over for him. Now, I need to ask you a question: can you teach Death, Dying and Religion?"

In a split second of spontaneous bravado (with no experience to back it up), I exclaimed "Sure!" I stood tall inside my certainty and, truth be told, I had no doubt. Besides, I had a whole summer ahead of me to prepare.

"Your new position," Benton said, "will be Full Time Temporary, which will be good for you. When another tenure track position opens, you should be in a good position to apply."

"Fantastic," I exclaimed, internally divided about just how "fantastic" it really was. And just that quickly, my mind shifted to practical matters.

"So you'll send me my schedule?" And he did, right away (two "Death, Dying and Religions," one "Western Religions," and one "Catholic Tradition"). With this boomerang—being let go and then brought back full time—my career at SJSU began. And it continued with the unexpected support from a wonderful woman, without whom I wouldn't have been able to make it all work.

"The Castilian Rose"

My Wonderfully Academic Daughters,

You'll remember Linda. My book, *Death Dreams: Unveiling Mysteries of the Unconscious Mind,* was dedicated to Linda, "A Castilian Rose where no others bloom." Not only did she type it for me, but she cared for you girls when I brought you to night classes at SJSU.

How it happened, I don't remember, but there she was—Linda Garcia (later, Garcia-Young)—a secretary in the social science dean's office, where religious studies teachers went for office supplies, coffee, and to use the photocopy machine. We talked. We talked about her two boys who, at the time, she was raising by herself. We became immediate friends. When she discovered I was a two-finger typist, she began helping with my manuscripts and other university-related work.

Without her loving support, my teaching career would not have happened as it did. She guided me, prepared dossiers, and typed manuscripts, letters, articles, and books for me on her own time. Without her steady assistance, I could not have made it through the tenure track maze.

I haven't, and couldn't, say enough about the tireless effort Linda spent helping me. Once, for instance, she encouraged me to apply for one of the California State Teacher-Scholar awards, which I then received. Funny how proud that little piece of paper made me feel, being acknowledged by my peers as one of the best at what I do.

When I completed my first serious book manuscript, *World Scriptures* (also typed by Linda), I sent it out to several presses with no luck—until, one day, I received a call from a Santa Clara Professor, Boo Riley.

"Hey Ken," he said, "a book representative from Paulist Press was just here looking for an introductory text to World Religions. I told him about you and your manuscript. He was very interested and wants you to send it to him."

"The Castilian Rose"

Not only was he interested, but also Doug Fisher at Paulist became my editor for that book and the two that followed.

It is impossible for me not to pause here and bow before the universe with profound gratitude for its overwhelming generosity. The calling that was leading me along my path and the responses that were rising up from my heart were aligning themselves perfectly. What can I say? What can be said? What would you girls say?

"You No Longer Need to Sit"

My Patient and Loving Daughters,

After landing in the mountains of Santa Cruz, settling in Brookdale (across from The Brookdale Lodge), it wasn't long before I heard about and began attending the Santa Cruz Zen Center, which was led by Kobun Chino Sensei. What a powerfully insightful, seriously joyous teacher. So I began attending his weekly talks.

The diminutive, black-robed, Japanese Buddhist sat *zazen* and gave *dharma* talks in the zendo around the corner from Holy Cross Church. Kobun brought Zen alive for me, making it practical and stirring buried insights.

When I first met him face-to-face, my head was over-filled with Rinzai Zen teachings, from Nishida, Nishitani, and Hisamatsu as taught by Richard DeMartino. I thought that *Awakening awakening to itself* was "Pure Zen," until I realized that Kobun, a Soto Zen practitioner, didn't ask about any of it. He was about "just sitting," just being fully yourself in this moment.

Kobun was a renegade, a maverick Buddhist, constantly tailoring his teachings to individual students. He was to Zen what Steve Jobs was to computers. In fact, Kobun was Jobs' spiritual teacher.

So I began practicing Zazen (seated Zen) under his tutelage. Week after week, forty-five minutes of silent sitting was followed by a Dharma talk.

It was the sitting that challenged me the most, a same difficulty I had already faced in a ten-day Vipassana meditation course in India with Goenka. With too much leg cramping and too little focus, I only lasted two days.

One evening, after I had been sitting and listening to Kobun, he met me outside the Zendo. Recognizing my difficulties practicing *zazen*, he told me: "You no longer have to sit." Alright! That released me from ever needing to sit *zazen* again, and I didn't. Actually, it released me from Zen as a

"You No Longer Need to Sit"

form of Buddhism, and I would soon come to realize the profound value of this.

When I was first getting to know Kobun, I was invited to attend a talk that he was giving at Saratoga Park. After the talk, he took out his calligraphy brush and scripted a message on calligraphy paper. When he looked up, he peered up directly at me and handed it over.

It turned out to be four lines from the "Cold Mountain" poem by Han Shan, a Chinese Zen master. "Wasn't he the Zen monk who's pictured riding on the back of a water buffalo while playing his flute?" I wondered.

Years later, Professor Chris Jochim and his wife Bau Chin gave me an almost literal translation of the four lines Kobun had written:

> I live in the mountains
>
> Nobody knows me
>
> Within white clouds
>
> Often silent and alone

At first, it seemed like a perfect depiction of Kobun himself—no one really knows what he is thinking. But then, another thought showed up. I wondered, *what if Kobun wanted me to try on Han Shan's poetic clothes, those of the anonymous monk who is often silent and alone?* A monk of no tradition; a monk of the universe. A finger seemed to be pointed at me and by someone asking the question, "Are you my teacher or are you my student?"

Then, in 2002, when Kobun took his family to vacation in Switzerland, as his young daughter was enjoying herself swimming in a lake, the unthinkable happened. Suddenly, she was no longer visible. Kobun instantly dove into the cold, dark, blue water to rescue her. Could he still see her? Would he have a chance to find her?

Neither of them surfaced; neither breathed again.

What were his final thoughts?

When I interviewed him about death in 1992 at SJSU, here's the way the interview concluded:

Kramer: *What is it like to be self-confident in the face of death?*

Kobun: I haven't experienced it yet. But with an eight-year old mind, I observed those people. All of them became holy creatures in my eyes because of how they suffered. In a few seconds, their faces changed, their bodies relaxed, they became very peaceful. I will prepare myself for this.

How so Kobun? Let's say that your bodily sensations told you that you were going to die soon. Would you do anything differently than you are doing now? Would you live your life any differently or practice any differently than you are practicing now in order to get ready for death?

Practically nothing will change, though I should go back home to pick up the mess I made. (Laughter). Sitting is a wonderful preparation for death. In the last moment of sesshin, breath goes and then you pass on.

Thank you, Kobun. We bow to you.

Kobun was simply a beautifully soft-spoken man.

Girls, what happened to Kobun in Switzerland makes me small. Once, when I asked him, "What happens when you sit?" he answered: "When I sit, the world sits."

Oh how I wish I had asked my respected teacher, in response, "What about when I die? What does the world do? Does the world die, too?"

Kobun, my friend, where are you now?

Holy Trinity Brothers

My Spiritual Daughters,

Catholic: why Catholic?

The Catholic possibility (or should I say my Catholicism?) first blossomed before my eyes when I met the non-canonical Anglican brothers of the Community of the Holy Trinity. Just four years after I landed in California, a new phase of my spiritual life began.

One sunny afternoon in a health food store in Soquel, CA while shopping for a tuna fish sandwich on rye with extra sprouts, extra lettuce and extra tomatoes, I saw three pale, white men in long black robes walking through the store. This was in the late 1970s, when spiritual journeyers were expressing themselves in eccentric forms of garb and practice. Probably because of the relaxed state of mind I was in, I walked directly up to one of the three, Brother William, and asked him, "What order do you represent?"

"We're Benedictine monks," he responded.

Each of them wore long, black robes with prayer beads encircling their waists and hanging down to the side, a cross at the end. "Our monastery is nearby," he continued, "if you would ever be interested in paying a visit."

"Certainly," I said. "Tell me when and tell me where."

Who were these guys? They wore long, black habits, sported closely shaved heads, and had vow crosses around their necks. The brothers were also caretaking an abandoned Catholic high school that was sitting on three hundred acres, with a magnificent view of the Pacific Ocean, behind Soquel Avenue in Santa Cruz.

When I first began visiting the brothers, they invited me into their small chapel for evening prayers. The majority of the service was chanted, which, for me, was the purest form of Benedictine Catholicism. Chanting

III—Traveling West (1974-2000)

engaged my whole being, relaxed and centered me, and prepared me to really listen in prayer. Soon, I began making several visits per week.

Anyone who stepped into their converted, hauntingly beautiful chapel felt its profoundly quiet spiritual energy. "Everything about it," a professor from UCSC wrote, "the chapel, the choir stalls, the library, the icons, bespeaks a holy order which bestows upon all who visit the place a real blessing of peace."

It was at this time (when you girls were around six and four) when your mother and I began talking about how you were going to be raised religiously.

Gaelyn agreed with me that you girls were to be raised religiously (with the caveat that it would give you both something to rebel against later on) as long as I was responsible for taking you where you needed to be taken.

I was completely willing to support Gaelyn's raising you girls Jewish if she wished.

"No way!" she said. Then what? Certainly not Baptist.

I had increasingly realized that a Buddhist I was not, however. I didn't have the fortitude, or the quiet center necessary for Zen practice.

It certainly surprised my non-practicing Jewish (second) wife when I told her that I was going to raise you girls Catholic. "I married a Buddhist, not a Catholic," she laughed, clearly insinuating that she far preferred the former to the latter.

I soon discovered that the The Holy Trinity Brothers enjoyed, as I did, moments of "herbal enhancement." After singing evening prayers, we would retreat to the common room, get uncommonly elevated, and then delve deeply into theological dialogues, that would eventually lead me to visit the new Camaldolese monastery in Big Sur. After spending several weekly retreats there, it became obvious to me that it was time to enter into the "one holy Catholic and apostolic" church.

More than anybody, it was Brother William who pointed me toward a new day. Having done time in Texas for burglarizing churches, he surprisingly converted to the Episcopal Church and then to Catholicism. In our challenging and stimulating talks, the charismatic Brother continuously motored between the intersection of madness, insight, and creativity. With a neatly trimmed mustache, balding naturally (except for the two-inch shaved strips of hair encircling his head from ear to ear), behind wired-rimmed glasses, he looked out with piercing eyes.

He didn't miss a thing, but neither did he comment on everything he saw. Brother William was convincing, deconstructing, and dialogical. He often took us into three or four steps of disagreement only to fly away into a highly creative construction, with old language used in new ways. It sometimes sounded, when he spoke, like you were overhearing a spontaneously written letter or a tightly scripted email riddled out as if from a page of literature.

Influenced by *The Rule of St. Benedict*, Brother William, as an Anglican, formed the Community of the Holy Trinity (CHT), along with Brother Lewis and Brother Patrick. At a time when new monastic communities were springing up across the country, CHT started with a prophetic vision based on their prison ministry in Soledad, CA, which was the most populous state prison in the country. Brother Lewis, the Catholic Chaplin's assistant at Soledad, provided music for the religious services there (Catholic and Protestant), recorded with inmates, and produced a gospel choir.

Later, the Anglican Brothers collectively became Catholics. This happened after they had been providing a twenty four-hour vigil for a Poor Clare's sister, Rose, who was dying of cancer. Her extraordinary devotion to God throughout the dying process converted each Brother to the Catholic faith.

The community gave presentations at UCSC and SJSU, and once offered a one-day interreligious symposium in the form of a dialogue between and among Fr. Bruno Barnhart (then the prior of the Camaldolese Monastery in Big Sur), Professor Ramundo Panikkar (internationally respected Hindu-Catholic Priest and author of many interreligious books), Professor Donald Nicholl (author and head of Tantur Ecumenical Center in Israel), and Brother William.

What finally brought me into the Catholic Church (for the next twenty-five years) was its practice of Eucharistic Sacramentality—especially as this Sacramentality has been understood by Benedictine monks. The reason is vitally simple—eating the resurrected body of Christ, *not his proteins*, is both an eternal and a temporal act. I needed a non-dualistic structure like this to ground my spiritual practice.

All of these changes—this re-grounding vision—provided me with a new stand, and a new direction.

"In Catholicism, the liturgical focus shifts from the efficacy of the preached word to the efficacy of the sacraments, from the persuasive power of the homiletician to being in the presence of the risen Christ," Brother William said.

You girls may be wondering what it meant for *me* to be Catholic.

Catholicism meant joining an unbroken historical succession of Christianity leading to the doorway of the original church. After studying the living religious traditions, it became clear to me that ritual was the most important aspect of most of these traditions. I wanted to align myself with the Catholic Eucharist because it was, for me, the ritual of rituals, the way ahead.

October 11th

Faithful Daughters,

I was sitting in a nondenominational church on 41st Avenue, five years after moving to Brookdale, and three years after buying a one-bedroom house beside a creek in Soquel. Holding a cube of communion "wonder bread" in my right hand, I heard the silent words of an invisible speaker: "Get to the Eucharist; get to the Eucharist." It was like suddenly hearing, on Pentecost Sunday, 1979, Bach's full throttled Toccata and Fugue in D minor on the organ.

I skipped to the nearest pay phone as soon as the service was finished, dropped a dime in, and dialed Brother William: "Welcome me," I said, "I'm Catholic!" Brother William was elated! I had become a Post-Vatican II-Catholic, which, my mother understood, but which dad never did.

Brother William knew I never felt myself to be a pious, parish Catholic. There was no way that I could "just" be Roman Catholic by itself. When people asked me, "What are you, Kramer?" a shiver would run up my spine. I would never say, "I'm a Roman Catholic." That would cause the earth to open up and swallow me. Instead, along with Max Mueller, who said, "If you know only one religion, then you know none," I began describing myself as "an interreligious Catholic," or as "a non-Catholic Catholic."

Since I was already baptized in a Christian church, I did not need to be re-baptized, and since I had been studying with Brother William and had received two theological degrees along with a doctorate in Comparative Religious Studies, no further instruction was required. The church held her arms wide open. There were no obstacles. The next time Father Bruno will be here will be on October 11th. This, as it happened, was the date on which Vatican II began in 1962, and, as I would later learn, was observed as St. Kenneth's Day on the Catholic Liturgical calendar.

"How's that date?" Brother William asked on the phone one day.

III—Traveling West (1974–2000)

"The sooner the better," I replied. So it was arranged.

Due to the west coast-east coast time difference, the morning Mass was at the same hour that my Easter baptism had been years before. I mention this because of a subtle connection between the two events that only afterward became obvious to me. This time, I entered the church in an all together new way. It was as if I was standing behind the mysterium instead of before it. It was as if I was inside an invisible set of gates looking out.

The "Rite of Reception of Baptized Christians into Full Communion with the Catholic Church" began after the homily, with an invitation to come forward and recite the creed with the faithful. Then, before friends and Gaelyn and you girls, I was invited to add, "I believe and profess all that the holy Catholic Church believes, teaches, and proclaims to be revealed by God." I was then instructed to kneel while Father Bruno laid his right hand upon my head and said,

> Kenneth Paul Kramer, The Lord receives you into the Catholic Church. His loving kindness has led you here so that, by the unity of the Holy Spirit, you may have full communion with us in the faith that you have professed in the presence of his family.

From the instant Father Bruno touched my head, I felt a new sensation of belonging resonate from my head to my knees and feet. Yet (why is there always a "yet" in the gap between anticipation and reality?), when I received my first Eucharistic body of Christ, it tasted no different than a matzah wafer, and the blood of Christ no different from ordinary red wine. Just like when I was baptized at Alpha Baptist Church, nothing changed in my perception of physical reality. No ecstatic zinger occurred.

October 11th

When I stood, I was greeted by each of the cloistered sisters who came one by one to the choir rail to touch my hands and heart. I was crying joyfully. The words of T.S. Eliot never made more sense:

> The end of our exploring
> Will be to have arrived where we started
> And know the place for the first time.

An only son, a North American Baptist, christened as an infant, fully immersed at thirteen, who had participated in and led college youth groups, had been an assistant minister and hospital chaplain in seminary, a spiritual pilgrim in India, and a Zen practitioner, I had now returned to the sacramental mystery of God's presence in the world.

I wept uncontrollably. The unconditional mystery of life was shining through the day again: God's immense and immanent grace.

I remember feeling like the final laborer who, in one of Jesus' parables, is given the same wage as a laborer who worked all day. I was given too much at thirty-eight, yet I could not have entered the fullness of the church

III—Traveling West (1974–2000)

any earlier. Perfect timing! I felt like a man or woman who had traveled through many cultures and beliefs, identifying with some along the way, who was returning home.

Although revolutionary for me, my entire Catholic experience left Gaelyn and me completely on different sides of the spiritual life. I had become a kind of anonymous monk, a person who seeks the presence of holiness—in both human being and in the Ultimate—by living a life of simplicity. In his monastic bible, *Blessed Simplicity*, Ramundo Panikkar described what he called the "new monk," an image I aspired to emulate, as someone who has felt called to live beyond what culture, even religious culture, allows. Gaelyn, by now, had become more New Age, and more Wiccan, more involved with channelers (especially Bashar), and, therefore, totally uninterested in Catholicism.

But what about you girls?

In a highly unusual ceremony, you were both baptized simultaneously by Father Watt on the porch of the Community of the Holy Trinity. This was performed at the behest of Brother William in order to allow you both to be received into the Catholic Church as immediately as possible. How fortunate (for you girls) that your father knew how to finagle his way to spare you from the Church's rigid rules!

Separation and Divorce

Beauties,

My life as PapaMa began when Gaelyn left me. To be fair, we had been discussing divorce for almost five years already. As I always said I would, I took complete responsibility for you, Leila, then nine, and you, Yvonne, then seven. At that moment, I vowed not to enter into another relationship with a woman for at least a year. That period of celibacy has extended to this day.

It may come to pass that the person who talks publicly and convincingly about love and marriage, will at times (often?) come later on to regret the enthusiasm of some of his or her words. I know because of a talk I once gave on "Living Love Fully" (imagine!) sometime after my first year of marriage to Gaelyn. The gist of what I said was that "true love" lasts forever. By "true love," I meant "unrelenting joy and happiness," which I knew because of my life-experience with her. And she, of course, in all her dazzling erotic beauty, was a member of the audience.

After the talk, a married woman in her late thirties/early forties came up to me and asked, "How long have you been married?"

"Almost a year," I said, "the most incredible year of my life!" Smiling all the while, she said, "You won't be able to give that talk in a couple of years. You'll see."

"Why not?" I inquired, disbelief oozing from my veins.

"Because life's challenges wear away at the strength of your love."

"That won't happen to our love," I assured her confidently, and I left feeling sorry for her. How could she not recognize the truth of my talk?

Years later, after we had moved to California and begun to raise you girls, our marriage began to decline. Gaelyn remained an exotically beautiful young lady—smart, creatively talented, and brimming with taste that always seemed ahead of others. Yet our differences continued to grow and our initial erotic passion was wearing thin. At one point, we tried an open marriage. It was an utter failure from my standpoint. Although she had no end of opportunities to satisfy herself (and took advantage of them), I experienced too much guilt and too much MS-libido to engage with other women.

And then we began attending a weekly meeting held by a wordless Guru, Baba Hari Dass, who communicated by writing short sentences on a chalkboard hung around his neck.

When your mother and I visited him—just the two of us—we told him that we wanted his advice about our marriage. Each of us said a few words about it. Then, writing on his chalkboard, he replied: "You reinforce each other's desires." We immediately assumed (or I did) that he was speaking positively about our relationship. It was only years later, after our marriage dissolved, that I realized it was just the opposite: desire is a trap. Non-attachment liberates.

During the last few years of our marriage, Gaelyn once astutely said to me, "We are just co-parenting." Her description of our marriage rang true to me. After our beach cottage on 13th Ave. burned down (what a gift Lottie Hullet made possible when she sold us her single-wall, redwood, one-bed cottage whose back door opened onto a deck which opened onto the sand), we bought a condo and retreated there. I had always said, when discussions of divorce arose, "I'll never leave the girls!"

Then, one lazy summer week, Gaelyn went to Oregon on a business trip with a man she would later marry. On the day before their planned return, I went to the 300-acre monastery where I ingested a tab of mescalin. Hours later, a bright sun broke its way through oak and eucalyptus branches as I found my way to a large sitting stone, from which I looked out onto the tree-filled acreage. Easily and naturally, I slipped into the Jesus prayer.

> "Lord Jesus Christ
> Have mercy on me
> A sinner."

With unmistakable clarity, there and then, I suddenly recognized that the time had come. The marriage was now complete. When Gaelyn would return, I'd say, "I'm taking the girls and we're moving." Where? I didn't have any idea. But I didn't care. As we both knew, the marriage was finished.

Around noon the next day, I was sitting at the dining room table facing the front door. You girls were playing upstairs. Suddenly, the front door opened. Gaelyn walked in filled with joy and happiness. "Ken, I want you to meet Bram. I'm going to move in with him!" Shocked and delighted at the same time, I quickly jumped up and extended my hand in friendship. With words marking a rite of passage I exclaimed, "Congratulations!" Heartily grabbing his hand, I continued, "She's all yours!"

Meanwhile, Gaelyn gathered some of her clothes, kissed and hugged you girls, and told you she was leaving but that she'd still be living in Santa Cruz. As quickly as she and I had moved in with each other, she and Bram left together.

Now what?

In a very short time, I felt that it was important to start a "new" three-person family unit. I sat you both down and explained to you that your mother had left. "It's up to us, now," I assured you girls, "and because it's only going to be the three of us from now on, let's make sure we have a good time!" So, with virtually no planning, I took you on a road trip to the San Diego Zoo and the Timkin Icon Museum.

I always felt good about the decision. There was no pain or fear associated with Gaelyn's leaving. I was just excited to raise you beautiful girls in a home where there would be no arguing, and no more discomfort.

How could I not raise you girls? How could I not be with my daughters all the time? And so I never remarried; in fact, I never dated again. Perhaps it was true, as a friend suggested, that MS had become my wife. One of the effects of my MS, it needs to be said, was a reduced libido. Besides, I had tried and failed marriage twice.

I often apologized to you, Leila and Yvonne, for providing such an imperfect role model with regard to marriage. For instance, I've never asked, "How did the fact that I never remarried affect you?" Maybe it wasn't the best thing I could have done. Do you remember when your mother left with much detail? Do you feel you missed out on the experience of a traditional, motherly role in your lives?

I could be a selfish asshole, as you girls know, but not selfish enough to think that my marriages failed because of Joanne or because of Gaelyn alone. No, just the opposite. In my recent conversations with you girls about your own relationships, when you assert, "If only he ... " and "If *only* he ... ." it's now far easier for me to recognize the fallaciousness of that kind of thinking than it used to be. It's not that I don't embrace the courage it takes to accept personal responsibility for my relational failures, but the other person is not blameless either.

Each relational situation calls for personal creativity, and if I ever hung a counselor-at-large shingle outside my door, it would read: "I'm the one who needs it."

In Each Other's Hearts

My Spirited Daughters,

"Dad, look!" Leila yells out to me with excited joy. I am in the kitchen of my parents newly-purchased stone house in Lower Trumbaursville, PA (near Quakertown) finishing breakfast and talking to my mother. You two are in the living room, kneeling on the brown couch and pointing out the window to the newly-fallen, white blanket of snow.

The day before, we had left sunny Santa Cruz for the Philadelphia airport, driving from there to North Philadelphia so that I could show you the brick row house where I was raised, and then continued on to my parents' house.

The next morning, the sheer stunning beauty of several feet of overnight snowfall lay on the ground. Its vast hush covered everything. The silent world was blessed by your first experience of snow.

"Daddy, look!" Yvonne yells with joyous excitement.

"Now you can see why I brought the sled with us. Let's get our flyer, warm clothes on, and go up to sled hill." "Sled hill" was a one-lane road that ran behind my parents' small acreage.

You could hardly wait. Grammy helped to squeeze you into warm pants, long sleeve shirts, sweaters, blue jackets, hats, gloves, and boots—like nothing you ever wore in Santa Cruz.

The door is opened. A cold gush of white glare rushes into the warm living room. The living room thermometer drops several notches. Grabbing the red-trimmed "flyer" sled (which I'd bought the summer before at the Santa Cruz flea market because it was just like the sled I had as a kid), I follow you both out the door. Too late. Before I can take pictures, each of you jumps off the four-step high concrete deck that grandpa had swept earlier in the morning, into the three feet of overnight snow.

In Each Other's Hearts

The newly fallen snow is as white as the ocean foam that you girls often run through at the Santa Cruz beaches. Here, there is no running; there is only thrashing about as you would in a pit of multi-colored plastic balls.

Was this just a fantasy? To be caught in the full sun of a blue sky day, in several feet of newly fallen snow, with ten-year-old Leila and eight-year-old Yvonne picking ice-fingers from low-hanging branches? If so, could any more magnificent fun be found?

Yet it is what happened next that none of us will ever forget.

Up the Trumbaursville road we walk, filled with anticipation, toward the hilltop. We speed in our black snow-boots, kicking up snow on each other as we hurry.

I had already told you stories of my sledding in the Philadelphia streets, of hiding behind cars parked near intersections and grabbing hold of their rear bumpers, to be pulled along on my sled down the street.

Now we are here. "Who's first?" I ask.

"Me!" "Me!" "Me!" "Me!"

So our first ride is me atop the sled, then Leila atop me, then Yvonne atop Leila.

Too much weight. The sled's runners dig into the snow-packed one-lane road. We are stuck.

Wasting no time, we unstick ourselves. First, two of us slide at a time; then, one at a time. "WEEEE!!" At times, one of you rolls off the sled and the "flyer" continues on down the hill. We yell; we scream; we cheer; we throw snowballs at each other. No time passes. Neither of you can wait. Each of you scamper back up, hugging the sled. When we are hungry, we simply backtrack.

Back home, Grammy is waiting with hot chocolate for everyone—you girls first, of course. Hot chocolate, then turkey and Swiss cheese sandwiches on rye.

We all sit at the kitchen table looking out the picture window across the snow-white field to the one-lane road where we had been sledding. That road preserves us in each other's hearts.

Halfway Between University and Church

My Devoted Girls,

After relocating to Santa Cruz, I hoped to find work at UCSC. Unfortunately, there was none, and they were in the process of dismantling their religious studies department. Our first year, there, in fact, was partially supported by unemployment insurance. Truth be told, I was enjoying our new location by the Pacific too much to want to interrupt its multiple pleasures. Plus, I had begun teaching courses at SJSU.

But you remember the real estate days. Before I was hired to a full-time position at SJSU, Gaelyn suggested that I obtain a real estate license, which I did, protestingly (after all, why should I have to give up my free time?). I took a "Real Estate Principles" course at Cabrillo Community College and passed the California State exam. I found a real estate office, began making phone calls, showing properties, closing escrows, and listing property.

Me—the PhD!

In two years, I had learned enough of the basics to become an investment broker—KRAMER REALTY. I rented a second floor office on 108 Locust Street no. 9, sat back, and waited. It didn't work. Either not much happened in spite of my efforts, or I didn't work at it with enough enthusiasm. So I shared my office with another broker.

One day, I said to him, "Kirk, perhaps you can help me locate a property. I'm looking for a house to buy for myself half-way between UCSC and Holy Cross Church." Within a month, Kirk told me he knew a realtor who owned a two-bedroom, one-bath, 800 square foot "fixer upper" on the upper west side. "She might want to sell," he said.

When I first saw the house, I knew it was a dream: a fixer-upper in a high-end neighborhood. Its owner, a realtor, knew that, too, and was asking an outrageous (or so it seemed to me) $135,000 for the house. Why outrageous? Because it was built on mudsills, had a septic tank, and a dirt driveway.

I was most attracted by the arbor, which was covered in purple wisteria and gold-yellow little roses in the quarter-acre yard surrounded by two five-acre parcels. When I showed the house and property to Deming Stout, a real estate investor, I said, "I'm not sure if I should buy it because there is so much that needs to be done to fix it up" to which he responded, "Kramer, if you don't buy this house, I will. Ken, this is what everyone wants." And that's why we're here.

A year later, I had saved enough money to lift the house from its mud sills with a series of car jacks, put in a concrete foundation, and set it back down on the new perimeter concrete foundation. Then, we built a two-story addition and doubled the square footage.

It was here that I raised you.

"The other day when I was in Portland on a business trip," Yvonne said, "as I was setting my alarm for the morning, suddenly the song you used to sing to us came back to me."

You sang, "It's time to get up; it's time to get up . . . You would stand at the bottom of the stairs and sing these words up to us every morning. You were our alarm clock."

It is here that I live now with you, Leila (and your family), and it is here that I hope to die.

From Crayons to Perfume

Endlessly Creative Young Ladies,

How glad I am that grandmom and granddad had a chance to see your early birthday booklets. As you know, these are booklets of your little poems, drawings, sayings, pictures, and stories, along with reflections that I wrote as you came of age. Year after year, I collected them in a folder tabbed with your names and forthcoming ages. I continued creating these birthday booklets for each of you, as you know, until you turned twenty-five.

Each year, I made enough booklets to send extra copies to family and friends. Recently, my artist friend, Robert Morgan, wrote, "I have been going through papers, including letters etc., for the Archives of American Art, and lo and behold, I found the complete collection of Kramer's magnificent chapbooks on his daughters in perfect condition."

To honor (definitely not to embarrass) you, here's one section from each of your youthful booklets and one from a booklet when you were in your twenties.

As I've told you, the booklets hold a treasure trove of great memories, the swell of love between words that "love you past infinity," as I used to say. And best of all a new photo, a new smile each booklet.

Here you are, Leila, at eight (can you even remember that far back?) when you caught me telling a fib as I remembered it in a poem:

Caught!

"It's you! I know!" Leila says.
"You are the tooth fairy!
I saw you put the money
under my pillow last time!"

"No; no!" Daddy says, "That
was because the tooth fairy
was late. It was the once
upon a time when daddy became
tooth-fairy-helper because
the tooth fairy had
too many stops to make before
morning, and we all know
what happens if tooth fairies
stay out past the rising sun!"
"No, daddy!
I saw you come in another time, too!"

I swear—you were one of the most creative eight year-olds I have ever met. Your intelligence baffled me, and your playful spirit kept me young. I'll never forget your messy auburn hair bouncing as you danced around the house on your tiptoes.

And here you are, Yvonne, at thirteen, coming into young womanhood, making a different kind of catch:

Foul Ball

Walking talking
in from the deck
Yvonne with Sommer
Next says: "Dad, Dad
wanna know what was
rad? I was sitting
in the stands eating
a burrito and I
saw this ball flying..."
(She points in the distance
and continues way more
calmly than she feels)
"So I put my burrito

III—Traveling West (1974–2000)

> down and reached out
> my hands like this Dad"
> (She unbends her right
> hand and lays it out
> in line with her waist)
> "And it plopped right in!"
> "Yeah" Sommer says,
> "She got up and reached
> her hand right out and
> it landed right in it!"
> "Yeah," Yvonne says,
> "And all the boys came
> running cause they wanted
> it cause of this . . ."
> Yvonne pulls a crumpled
> blue card from her jeans:
> "When you return a
> foul ball you get
> free ice-cream!"

Even at the young age of thirteen, you were a strong, and self-assured girl. You had no problems talking to strangers about your entire life story, and your innocent emerald eyes were always smiling, shining with determination.

Then, Yvonne, when you graduated from San Diego State University at twenty-two, I met one of your friend's mothers:

Soo Proud

> Hearing Her
> Mom
> Tell Me
> About You:
> Always
> So Respectful

So Up-beat

And Me

Soo Proud

By the age of twenty-two you had grown into a tremendously beautiful woman, and your heart was filled with nothing but love and appreciation for the world. Oh, how I love you.

And Leila, when you turned twenty-four, I spoke with one of your former professors:

Former Professor

Who,

Hearing,

Said:

"Every once

In a while

A student

(You)

Comes along

Who,"

He said,

"Is not only

Bright but"

—Yes—

"Exemplary

In every way."

How proud I was at the woman you became by twenty-four! You were strong-willed, and dedicated yet still filled with beauty and grace.

Watching the two of you grow through the teenage years and become young working women, was like finding new words filled with joy. We will always be connected through the words from these booklets, my loves.

The Faces of MS

Dear Merciful Daughters,

How easy it was to sail through the uncomplicated joyous waves of my first forty years. While I could, or should, have been scared by my diagnosis of MS, I wasn't. I felt healthy; I felt happy; and I felt worthy of both. Even though, always lurking in the background, was my dark secret, a midnight ocean wave influencing all aspects of my life more than I knew and more than I ever let on, it was easy for me to stand tall.

Girls, I know I didn't mention my disease much, especially when you were growing up. Acknowledging my condition always felt like admitting to a weakness that would negatively impact the way people related to me. So I hid. When I wasn't teaching, I rarely left the house, with the exception of academic research trips abroad (in the summers) and shopping, swimming, or worshiping. It was as if I was becoming a hermit in the world.

There were reminders that flared up and passed: moving furniture and losing movement in my right leg; puncturing my hand on the rusty back fence wire, which caused an infection, which caused a flare up; crying after returning from a spinal tap that confirmed the MS diagnosis; standing with wind blowing in my ear outside the County building when I was dealing with my parents' paperwork, which triggered an episode of full body numbness; after having a urological test that led to an infection that led to my needing a cane when walking; and in the midst of all of it, the neurologist proscribing an A.F.O. (ankle-foot orthotic) to help me with my drop foot, and on into my future use with a cane, a walker, and, finally, a motorized chair.

In the corners of my wonderment, I knew early on that these disabilities would come, like the week my right arm went numb and made it impossible to grip a pen to finish the chapter on Islam in my *Sacred Art of Dying* book. Separated by a year or two, flare ups emerged like a hurricane and then departed—relapsing and remitting—yet accompanying every remittance was a new diminishment, a former mobility taken away, a new immobility added.

Most of my difficulties have come when I've had to converse with other illnesses—most recently, trigeminal neuralgia. As if MS isn't devastating enough on its own, when MS plaque resides in the area of the brain through which the trigeminal nerve passes on its way to the face and jaw, electrical shocks are sometimes generated. They come and they go without warning. When here, they keep my heart racing anxiously. They make me—when they are firing—wish that my facial nerve were dead in spite of the numbness in my jaw that would come to exist for the rest of my life.

How did I process it emotionally? That's just it—I didn't. I buried my fears. I didn't discuss them. I didn't think about what could possibly happen. Why would I? MS left me without any control. It frightened me. I hid from it and hid it from others; hiding it became a lifestyle. I wanted no part of something that wanted every part of me. While I tried to remain positive, dark moments didn't disappear.

Yet, I would not, *could* not walk through any of these doors without you, my loving daughters, without the light shining from your eyes, without the music that our conversations gives us.

One morning, as I approach the health club, a woman in dark glasses passes me without pausing to hold the door open.

Inside, a tiny lady greets me with a bright smile.

"Hi Ken," she says enthusiastically. "Happy New Year." She continues down to the other end of the hall, pauses to peer into the cycling room, as if looking for someone, and then walks back.

"You made it down the hall and back," I say "before I could make it halfway down."

"Yeah, but you made it," she answers. "That's what counts. You're an inspiration to the rest of us." She smiles.

"I don't know about that," I say, "but I do know that the gift MS gives me is this conversation."

She smiles again, but this time her lips don't part as widely as they had before.

"By being forced to slow down," I continue, "I have the opportunity to engage with those who are able to slow down without being forced."

"This," I say, passing my open hand back and forth between us while holding on to my walker, "is a gift that we give each other."

III—Traveling West (1974–2000)

This time her smile was huge. Not only her lips, but her eyes and her cheeks and her eyebrows were all smiling.

"And I love your laughter," I say.

Later that morning, while sitting in my parked Jeep at the ocean, meditating on the waves rolling into the shore, I have three thoughts about my writing: 1) I have nothing worthwhile to say; 2) I don't know the best way to say it; 3) who cares? I recall the exasperation generated by the interplay of these three thoughts.

As I recall this, a seagull flies up from the beach, lands on the hood of my Jeep. It looks through the windshield at me. First, it looks with one eye and then it looks with both, turning its head from side to side. I notice an orange spot on both sides of its lower yellow beak. Wind pushing against its feathers, the gull turns and walks toward the windshield, as if to look and see what I'm doing inside. When it hops off the hood, it waits to see if I will throw any food from my window before hopping back up.

On the beach below, three teens chase each other.

I'm sure you girls remember me telling you this story soon after it happened. Now, I look back on that story through a different lens. Now, I can no longer drive for myself. Now, I have become totally dependent on others—a prisoner of my own devices.

My MS is stubborn. It disagrees with me wherever possible. It shows up in deconstructive, "this-again?" ways.

Now, I discover along with the multitudinous *visible* masks it wears, there's an *invisible* one. The trouble is, this invisible one only manifests when it's too late.

Why? Now that people with MS, because of ever-newer medicines, are living longer, they can expect older age to bring greater disability.

How does that invisible mask affect me? As I age, it will be difficult (if not impossible) to tell if what's happening (cognitive impairment, dysfunctional bowels, diminished balance, and got-me-on-my-knees anxieties) is because of MS or just because of aging.

So what! Like a bird flying into a window, I didn't see this next painful episode coming. So what? It's all MS. Do you know how going-down feels in those moments? There are many layers of going-down. I am scared, in those moments, and depressed.

"I" Exam

My Understanding Daughters,

Putting MS aside (again!), in this letter I'm sharing with you the invisible bars, that, for years, imprisoned me in false ideas that stole away my mind.

Something was missing in my life. It wasn't anything I could put my finger on. It certainly wasn't another idea, another book, another teacher, another another. That I knew. But what? That, I didn't know.

Not that I spent a lot of time worrying about what it was. By all accounts, life was going well. You girls were at UCSC (Leila) and SDSU (Yvonne). I was a published, full professor. Okay, there was my MS, but even that was being, somewhat, kept at bay by weekly injections of Avonex (an immune suppressant), swimming, a great diet, a positive attitude, and lots of sleep.

Still . . . .

For too long, especially in my Buddhist years (my late twenties and early thirties) and then in my Catholic years (my late thirties, forties and fifties), I believed (wished) that some event, some awakening would seize me and resolve my spiritual anxieties once and for all. This would allow me to execute a spiritual blueprint especially designed to remodel my soul. All that I had to do was find the right blueprint. You may already see *my* problem here.

But there are many "right" blueprints. What I had to do was to just execute one. Failing that, it became apparent that I would have to start creating the blueprint myself. At first, I had sought out peak experiences, even though Professor Donald Nicholl in the old city of Jerusalem during Christmas of '85 once warned against the blindness of collecting these "spiritual experiences." I read book after book by enlightened masters or grace-filled mystics even though Bodhidharma, the presumptive founder of Zen, taught its basic principles as:

III — Traveling West (1974–2000)

> Not relying on words or letters;
> An independent Self-transmitting apart from any teaching;
> Directly pointing to Heart/Mind;
> Awakening Original-Nature-actualizing Buddhahood.

As a late blooming hippie (though I never described myself that way), I tried applying transformational technologies from the human potential movement, to my life, but always with the same lack of success. Breakthroughs came, but they were followed (a week later, a month later) by the same breakdowns and the same anxieties I had felt before.

I sought out spiritual persons of intense interest (East and West) and interviewed them, later transcribing their words, putting some into books. Yet those words always remained someone else's insights, someone else's way.

I was looking in the *wrong places* for the *wrong thing* in the *wrong way*. In each situation, I remained separate and separable from the belief, from the practice. Whether Zen's no-self awakening, or Catholicism's living-and-dying with Christ, each remained stuck within the content of my own experience. I had overlooked, of course, Dogen's advice: "We do not work to support our practice, our work is our practice."

And yet I could not resist looking. Without consciously realizing it, my conundrum was relentlessly pointing me toward *relationships* and calling me to take the day by the hand and practice *genuine dialogue*.

"My mistake," I once said in a class where I guest lectured after retiring, "was not recognizing that 'I' had made a mistake from the beginning. My basic premise—my operational motive—was wrong. For the better part of two decades, across several continents, I was looking for what doesn't exist, pretending all the while that it did.

I was searching for 'self-awareness' as if such a thing, such a truth, such an enlightenment existed independently of myself, as if I could realize it for/by myself. I had interpreted the awakened self through egocentric categories without first letting my egoistic individuality morph into relational personhood.

I created my own conundrum as a consequence: to live in and overlook the problem until it was forgotten. I had forgotten the vital distinction between 'not knowing' and 'not knowing that I didn't know.' Forgotten, too, was the Bodhisattva's teaching: 'I will not enter Nirvana until all sentient beings enter Nirvana.'"

"I" Exam

After hearing me at SJSU about these wasted years, an innocent, enthusiastic, young man (an earlier me?) earnestly asked: "How can I avoid making your mistake?"

Wasting no words, yet full of hesitation, I said: "With the best intention, a little grace, and some luck." Even as I was saying this, I felt a gigantic NO arise in my consciousness. No, that's not right. There's no answer other than by making the mistakes yourself.

I shiver, now, recalling the sincere eyes and earnest voice of the questioner.

"Jesus, as a Jew, Would Never Have Said That"

My Considerate Daughters,

I first met Mishael Caspi (colleague, teacher, collaborator, and dialogical companion) on a fall Saturday morning in the mid 1980s in a dentist's reception office, where Mishael was offering weekly presentations on biblical stories. How to describe the silver-haired sage? In his late fifties, he speaks with a Yemenite inflection and gestures with a patriarchal, rabbinic flare. A storyteller, a lover of rose-fragrances, imposing, dark-skinned and passionate—extremely passionate.

Raised a North American Baptist and having completed four years of theological work and a PhD in Religious Studies, I was familiar with the stories he was telling. What was new—refreshingly so—was the combination of Mishael's passion for the textual narratives and his attention to the little-noticed details that brought a new understanding to the story.

I was, at the time, a Benedictine-influenced Catholic Oblate. In contrast, Mishael was born into an Orthodox Jewish family in Israel, was steeped in the literature of the Hebrew tradition, and eventually became a multi-linguistic scholar of Judaism, Christianity, and Islam.

He was the person I always called up when I had a question (whether mine or a student's) about Judaism. He knew the Biblical text in its original language along with early and traditional Rabbinic interpretations. What an incredible Buberian conversation we struck up: at the café, in classes, in his office at UCSC. Incredible. Mishael, a text, myself—we three, equal partners, equal voices.

Once, we offered a series of dialogical presentations at Holy Cross Church. That evening as we were discussing the Passover-Eucharist, Mishael suddenly said, "Jesus, as a Jew, would never have said, 'This is my body, this is my blood.'"

"Jesus, as a Jew, Would Never Have Said That"

I'll never forget the sudden illumination I experienced. "He's right," I remember thinking. There's no way that a Palestinian Jew in the first century of the Common Era following Kosher law would ever have identified himself literally with the blood and the flesh that was about to be consumed.

Given the centrality of these words to the Catholic liturgy, Mishael's understanding with its radical common sense, rearranged the certainties I had in my tradition. His interpretation had a profound effect on me as a Trinitarian Catholic sacramentalist.

"What do you think Jesus might have said instead?" I asked him.

Mishael remarked, "As a parablist, Jesus could have said, 'This is like my body.' It is a Passover custom," Mishael continued, "after the service is finished and food and drink have been consumed, for guests to have an opportunity to speak their interpretation of the *Seder*."

I remembered nothing more, except that the Eucharist was never the same for me. Now, it was re-contoured with a single interreligious, Jewish-Catholic, deconstructing/reconstructing brushstroke. A pillar of my practice had been transfigured. No longer could I coast through Mass with my eyes half opened.

Now, when I heard the priest quoting Paul's version of what Jesus is reported to have said, my mind and spirit were awakened to another, a Jewish interpretation, one that penetrated my Eucharistic prayers and silences.

Girls, this was a necessary steppingstone along my journey, like one of those "The Childhood Door," and "The Materializing Guru," moments. But this time it was triggered by dialogue instead of a "mysticism of the particular" as Maurice Friedman would say.

This time, instead of searching for something, I was found by what I wasn't looking for. What a far-reaching moment—it was the beginning of the end of organized religion for me.

You knew Mishael and his wife Gila as beautiful people. When I would thank Mishael for everything he's taught me, he would say, "My brother, your questions milk me. They bring out the best in me." Such beautiful honesty.

In my life, I have met less than a dozen men (younger and older) to whom I truly feel close. Mishael was my only brother.

The Divine Comedian

My Lighthearted Beauties,

It was Mishael who told me about Dr. Emilio Dido, the eighty-year-old blind Italian Catholic doctor who treated patients with injections of ionized distilled water twice a day at his medical clinic. I had tried other alternative approaches to mitigate MS's diminishments (acupuncture, various diets, and shiatsu massage) with no effects, but in the summer of '93, off I went to Rome to try another one.

Did I believe I'd be cured, even partially? No. Still, I suppose I'd be disingenuous if I said I had no hope. Also, I was interested to meet the eighty-year-old doctor who I would eventually call "the divine comedian."

What happened? Not much, physically. After fifteen days of twice-daily infusions of the specially-charged water, all that happened was that my involuntary spasticity subsided. That's it. Spiritually, however, Dr. Dido gave me a gift I still appreciate. It may not seem like much to you girls. It didn't get my attention at first either. It happened in one of our side conversations. During my time there, on a three day trip to and from Assisi, several hours north of Rome, we had many opportunities for short conversations, as well as a few longer talks.

One afternoon, Emilio invited me to into his office. Knowing of our mutual interest in Catholic mystics and of his dedication to St. Francis, I asked him about his own spiritual practice. I was hoping to hear something I had never heard before. Did I!

"Prayer, prayer, and more prayer," he responded, "morning, noon, and night. Especially at night. Whenever I can't sleep, or wake up in the middle of the night, I sit on the side of my bed and pray." What I didn't know at the time is that he had just given me what no one else on earth ever had given me. Without willing it, led by the force of habit, I reached out and shook his hand. "Thank you," I said, "thank you."

The Divine Comedian

While I didn't think about it much after that, over the years I have adhered to his practice, with only one exception. When I wake up in the middle of the night, I remain in bed. I invite the Superaddressee (whom most Jews, Christians, and Muslims still call God) to hang out for awhile until I can fall asleep again. It's a different kind of praying, an overlapping weave of rhythmic breathing, relaxed rememberings, and improvisational thinking. At times, like a dream, an insight-narrative shapes itself in response to my prayer's silent rhetoric.

Now—spending twelve hours in bed each night as I do—the Ultimate Listener has become my nightly companion. On the opposite wall from my bed hangs an Egyptian Coptic icon of Jesus (one that I brought back from Jerusalem), his hands surrendered upward in prayer. At night, when I wake, I fix my gaze on his fixed gaze and attune my spirit to the eternal Thou.

Girls, you must know by now, through the years that the two of you are at the very top of my list of persons to pray for—whether for your safety, your specific needs, your situational issues, your health, your family, your accomplishments, or your relationships—I am continually praying for you both. As for me, I might pray something like:

> Father All-Mighty, Earthly Mother have mercy on me. Please Lord of all, accept even these wandering thoughts that weave themselves into my intentions, especially for Leila and Yvonne, for Sienna and Grayson, and may I continue to be attentive to Your voice, to Your signals, to the way You respond. I am not worthy and I need Your mercy to free me from my stupid self, to awaken me to what I can know of You. I gratefully, gratefully, gratefully bow to You.

The Right Question for the Wrong Person

Dear Yvonne Rose and Leila Ann,

If ever there were a chance for a breakthrough with my dad, it would have been this moment. Grandmom and Granddad had moved to California because they could no longer care for themselves. But neither could we take care of all their needs. That was beyond our abilities.

It was for this reason that, when I received a laudatory letter from the Dean of Humanities announcing that I had been promoted to full professor at SJSU, I was eager to show it to them.

A great sense of accomplishment swept over me. As you know, I came from parents who never finished high school, was published, and now was being promoted to full professor, one with an outstanding teaching record. Now there it was all there for the world to see.

So, on a fall afternoon, with bright sunlight glancing through the leaves, I drove to visit my parents in their tree-shrouded Assisted Living facility a few minutes outside of Santa Cruz. In my hand, I clutch my letter from the Dean, still in its original envelope, addressed to me.

We sit outside on the porch under the melody of chirping birds, the enveloped letter in my hand. An extra-bright smile describes my fifty-two-year-old face.

"This is it!" I say, holding the letter out. "I am now a full professor. This means that I have gone from assistant professor, to associate professor, and now to full professor (notice, with extra money)!"

I give the letter to them to read.

"Congratulations, Kenneth!" Grandmom says with a large smile and a gracious hug. "This is wonderful."

Then she turns to Grandad who has been silent throughout. She says, "Roy, don't you want to tell Kenneth that you are proud of him?"

The Right Question for the Wrong Person

The chirping birds suddenly left their branches and flew to another tree. Silence. Just as he never said "I love you" to me, he had never said that he was proud of me.

What my dad never knew—he never once asked about my teaching—was that it wasn't unlike being a preacher-man. Look: I was teaching religious texts, as interpreted by humanist-existential teachers, as taught by a believing phenomenologist (me). At times, when appropriate, in order to awaken unthinking students, I even talked excitedly like a preacher inflecting his voice to make a significant point.

My mother's question echoes, but there is still only silence. Are you proud of me yet?

And the time you hit me, and the time you killed the kitten, and the times you embarrassed me at Church insisting on calling me "Kenny" into my late teens, and all the times you didn't play ball with me like other kids' dads, are all given over into that silence.

I know no way of compensating for this silence. Its burning numbness has locked me up. I wonder how you would have felt, Dad, if I had instead been a thief, a thug, or a fakir? Or could I only ever be half right—if that—with you?

Girls, you can feel some of the pain between two proud men that still exists in me to this day. But what was he thinking?

When I look at this moment through his eyes, I can see resentment simmering beneath the surface. How did it make him feel to see his son, given all the advantages that he himself never had, succeed? It was his dedication to a life of five-day-a-week work that made education possible for me. And then, I didn't become the preacher he wanted to become. I wonder, if I had become that man, would he have been able to muster up those encouraging words?

What if . . . ?

What if this episode asks the right question of the wrong person?

Oh, if only I had the miraculous grace in that bird-chirping fall afternoon to intercede for your Granddad and respond to Grandmom's question, "Aren't you proud of him?" myself—"Yes, I know that he is, mom." And then, turning to my father, I'd say "And I am proud of you, Dad, of all you have done for me! I couldn't have been as successful without you. Thank you, Dad."

Teaching on the Narrow Ridge

My Studious Daughters,

To think that I once brought you to a class at SJSU! I wanted you to see me doing what I loved doing—teaching. It was there that I could be free, innovative, and happy. I want to include, therefore, this little essay written for the SJSU Newsletter in which I briefly describe how to teach dialogically:

> *Teaching on the Narrow Ridge*
> By Kenneth Kramer
> Teacher Scholar 1994-1995

> *We walk on a narrow rocky ridge between the gulfs where there is no sureness of expressible knowledge but the certainty of meeting what remains undisclosed.*
>
> Martin Buber

Teaching on the Narrow Ridge

Eleven years of undergraduate and graduate studies, plus twenty-five years of university teaching, have shown me that no matter how brilliant the professor, how fascinating and valuable the course, the learning-teaching process, at its best, is a function of *dialogical attentions*. Like it or not, if students are to be excited by the significance of the subject matter, its presentation, its articulation, its enactment itself must be exciting. Does this suggest that a teacher should be passionate about the course? Yes. But even more importantly, it suggests that the overall course methodology itself must be interactive to engage the student's attention.

1.

Alright, I say with a sly grin, now let's shift our attention to *how* this course will be taught. Since asking generative questions (questions that evoke further questions) is integral to the course, let us begin with one that at first may sound a bit strange. How can we symbolize the teaching-learning process?

Looking back over my shoulder (and exclaiming, with Confucius, "What greater Joy!") I choose three metaphors from the writings of the philosopher of dialogue Martin Buber because they trace my own development as a teacher. Admitting that, as a colleague has informed me, I am a meaning-junkie, I offer these reflections knowing full well that, in the end, it is the relationship of real mutuality that provides the essential context in which the educational process flourishes. In a reciprocal classroom, the teacher and the course material come alive with a personal immediacy that draws the students forth.

2.

Buber characterizes contrasting approaches to education with three suggestive images. The metaphor of the funnel, for Buber, reflects a mostly traditional view of education. In a funnel approach to teaching, the teacher (the one who knows) pours the material under study into the receptive minds of students. This image, emphasizing the importance of an objective education, characterized my early teaching. I remember spending hours researching, assembling, and typing forty-five minute lectures to be read in detail. How else could one be expected to cover the required information?

However, long before the advent of computers, I realized the futility of this approach, not to mention its lack of spontaneity and freedom.

The metaphor of the pump, for Buber, reflects a more progressive view of education. In this approach, emphasizing the subjective side of knowledge, a teacher's role is to facilitate the unfolding potentialities within their students. Following psychologists like Carl Jung and Ira Progoff, who maintain that the deepest spiritual wisdoms of humankind remained stored as images and symbols in the collective unconscious, I have encouraged students to create their own scripture-like passages by imitating the style of existing texts (or to write their own messages by imitating what a past master teacher would say today). Over the years, though, I came face to face with the limitations of this approach as well. Combinations of ineptness, ignorance, and laziness (on both sides of the teaching-learning curve) sent me searching for a more organic methodology.

A third metaphor, the metaphor of the narrow ridge, expresses for Buber a kind of teaching that does not rest on the broad upland of "sure statements" or of "sure knowledge" but instead on a dialogical ridge between the either-ors of the intellectual world. Neither the teacher-oriented (the funnel), nor the student-oriented (the pump) pedagogy, for Buber, generates the kind of genuine teaching and learning that occurs through real meetings on the narrow ridge of engaged relationships.

In this approach, teaching and learning conversations flow between unique persons in an *I-Thou* structure of honest openness that preserves, yet dynamically overcomes, their separateness. Simply put, genuine dialogue cannot be located within any one of the participants, but rather is found in their "between-ness," in what Buber calls the reality of the "interhuman." Accordingly, the basic movement of genuine dialogue, and thus of education itself, is a truly reciprocal conversation in which teacher and students are full partners.

3.

Consider here, for example, a study of 125 biographies of prominent Americans. Over and over again, three characteristics were given to depict an effective teacher: 1) subject-matter competence; 2) caring deeply about each student; and 3) expressing a unique passion or eccentricity. It is the second characteristic that designates what occurs on the narrow ridge of genuine dialogue, from the teacher's side. How does one proceed with this methodology? How does a teacher cultivate a deep caring for students?

Effective teaching, I believe, establishes an open context for the emerging potential presence of each person by encouraging reciprocal conversations between a teacher and students. In this kind of learning community, students are affirmed as unique persons who bring distinctive experiences to the classroom. Teachers, by boldly swinging over to the student's side of the relationship, imagine what students are thinking, feeling, and experiencing. And students, in the process, are invited to interact with the teacher and with the subject-matter by entering the educational conversation without restraint.

I know, girls, that this approach might not be like those used in classes that you've taken. Yet, can you imagine exciting possibilities for yourself resulting from practicing this overall methodology in your careers? You know the main ingredients by now: enthusiasm, clarity, listening, and creative dialogues beginning to end.

The Limits of Dialogue

Dialogical Daughters,

In the mid 1990s, I was elected (along with a half-dozen other professors at SJSU) as a teacher/scholar for a year. We were each asked to write a brief teaching statement. Mine was:

> My premise is that it is not the teacher who educates the students; rather, it is the relationship between them in their encounter with each other and with the material that creates an active learning community. My primary educative tool, therefore, is dialogical reciprocity: the ongoing dialogue I have with my own teachers, with my students, with the course materials, and with myself in response to the learning process.

Having said this, I am quick to recognize that the entire process of entering into genuine dialogue with another is predicated upon one's ability to turn away from one's self and then towards the other with one's whole being, to turn toward a deep, interhuman exchange.

The Limits of Dialogue

I once invited Maurice Friedman to visit my classes at State to speak about dialogue. At a significant moment in our exchange, I said, "What is needed is an awareness that truly considers every person in their particular situation. But, there are limits."

In response, he said:

> There are several limits [to dialogue]: one is time; one is hunger; and one is that you do what you can in a situation. There are even tragic situations where there are simply not enough resources on either side for a genuine meeting to take place. You don't insist on the dialogue and you don't assume it will always happen—you are simply open for it. If I could make dialogue happen, that wouldn't be dialogue. That would be willfulness. So I have my radius. I can prevent it, though. There can be a one-sided prevention of dialogue. I can do it simply by saying—"nothing's going to get through to me." But when there's a willingness for dialogue, then—and you used the word earlier—one must "navigate" moment-by-moment. It's a listening process.

Here lies the brilliance of dialogue's response-generating response. *It's a listening process.*

Yet, how do I deal with those who aren't interested in being dialogical? It's simple. If I am not really interested in the person or topic, I withdraw my energy. However, if I am, I keep asking thought-provoking questions hoping to draw the otherness of the other into an open conversation. But then, as Maury says, "It's a listening process"—on both sides.

"The Search Will Make You Free"

Yvonne and Leila,

Here's the other side of dialogical limitations. Just as I would say that my master teacher is Martin Buber, my good friend from graduate school, Harold Kasimow, a self-confessed "Jewish pluralist" for whom religious diversity is the will of God, would say that his master teacher is Abraham Joshua Heschel. He actually knew Heschel and had conversations with him as a student.

In one sense, our teaching and writing have directly carried forward each of our teachers' teachings. In fact, they have often been compared. They are certainly similar in the dialogical domain, just as I am, on a personal plane, with Harold.

Realizing, with Buber, that the presence of "genuine dialogue" cannot be fully conveyed by conceptual language, allow me to offer, by way of example, an event that embodies the working of its spirit. In one of my conversations with Kasimow, an incident occurred that might be described, in the spirit of Buber's metaphor, as a moment of sacramental dialogue.

Like myself, Harold was a professor of comparative religious studies and interested in various forms of interfaith dialogue. Our conversations in the past had been marked by a frank mutuality of the kind not always present between persons. One day, after discussing a book review that he wanted me to write related to my interest in Mahayana Buddhism, I asked him about his current writing projects. He had just completed a book of essays on interreligious dialogue that he was planning to send to his publisher the following week.

In a voice that carried both concern in the face of what was still unfinished and pride in what he had accomplished, he said, "I need a title!" When he told me his working title—*Singing a New Song: A Jewish Dialogue with World Religions*—I impulsively, but confidently, replied that the

"The Search Will Make You Free"

subtitle described the book's purpose precisely, but that the main title (since its purpose was to catch the potential reader's attention) was dissatisfying. He agreed.

After I indicated that I would take some time to think about his problem, an idea, at first not fully formed, urged itself upon me. Recalling how we often spoke fondly of our now dead professor from graduate school, Bernard Phillips, who had set each of us on the interreligious path, I asked him a rhetorical question: "Who was your favorite grad school professor?" When he answered "Professor Phillips," I asked him another question, the answer to which I thought I already knew:

"And what is your favorite essay of his, the one that you include in the reader you assemble for your students?"

"The Search Will Make You Free," he responded.

As if addressing the continuum of his teaching and writing career, I said, "*There's* your title!—*The Search Will Make You Free: A Jewish Dialogue with World Religions*."

In the silence that followed, I felt a sense of acceptance sweeping over him. Not only did the new title accurately describe the book's contents, but it also honored the professor who most influenced the writing of the book.

"That's perfect!" he said, excited, as I was, by the mutual gift we had just received.

So you see, in moments, though they may be rare, when words become bouquets of flowers, and flowers, rainbows, people are genuinely connected.

What's Missing?

My Trusting Daughters,

One sunny, summer afternoon, I began thinking of my "Death, Dying, and Religions" course, which I had taught (two sections each semester) at San Jose State for more than a decade. I was daydreaming about how the course could be advanced. How could my presentation of the material be rethought in a way that would liberate both the teaching and the studying of death and dying? How should the death event be thought of?

It occurred to me that across many academic fields, including education, there exists a universal difficulty when people communicate, one that drives a seemingly impenetrable wedge between persons—namely, the lack of real dialogue.

I decided to enliven my classes by inviting so called "death experts" to come and be interviewed. To make it easier for students to connect with the various speakers, I indicated to them ahead of time that I would begin each interview with this question: "What's missing from most people's understanding of death and dying that prevents them from having a richer, deeper insight into the experience?"

The Swiss-born psychiatrist, Elisabeth Kübler-Ross, was the first professional in the field anywhere to really listen to the voices of dying patients and to give them a public forum. Her five stages of death and dying—denial, anger, bargaining, depression, and acceptance—have become universally known. In our interview, she directly connected the acceptance of death to an individual's sense of spirituality.

Kramer: The first question I would like to ask you, Elisabeth, is a question that I have asked each of the people that I have interviewed: What do you think is the missing element in the way that people respond to death and dying, the lack of which keeps them from having a healthier attitude toward death?

What's Missing?

Ross: They have no evolved spiritual problem. If they have any spiritual sense, they are in touch throughout the living world with their soul. They will know that dying is nothing to be afraid of. They are afraid to look inside, they are afraid to look to what God is all about. They don't know anything about human evolution. They worry about taxes, making a living, getting through the year, or a tax year, or whatever, and they don't go beyond that. They are like in kindergarten. And then those human beings who are in kindergarten should not worry about those things, because they are not there yet. That's where evolution takes place. When they finally begin to worry about it, they get excited, [. . .] and then their spiritual quadrant opens and then they ask the right question and then they get the answer. You just have to ask and you find out. But you have to be at a certain level of evolution to even consider that.

Next was Ram Dass, also known as Richard Alpert, a professor of psychology and the author of the highly influential book, *Be Here Now*. In it, he takes readers on a journey into the heart of Hindu spirituality and addresses the importance of being fully present in each moment.

Kramer: What do you think is missing from most ordinary conversations about death and dying? And by that I mean: What's missing, say, the presence of which would enable human beings to be more creative in the face of death?

Ram Dass: What's usually missing from dealing with death and dying in our culture is that we take our separateness seriously, as absolute reality. We really think we're "somebody." And if you're somebody, you're absolutely going to die. We don't recognize the other planes of consciousness in which we aren't separate entities. There are equally real planes in which we are simply awareness, which has nothing to do with birth and death. Births come and deaths come, and on it goes, and insofar as "awareness" is concerned, you are still right here.

With birth and early childhood, you go into "somebody" training; then you start taking yourself seriously; and you cultivate your somebodyness, and go to San José State and become somebody special. And then, with grace, you start awakening, and realize, "God, did I get trapped in that dream!" And you start to wake up and see that you are really something much more vast than even that special somebody. You are just living out this particular sequence, this dream sequence. And that's all that dies—the dream sequence. You as awareness don't die.

III — Traveling West (1974–2000)

That's what's missing, for the most part, in the death and dying literature.

If you trace where we come from in our ideas about death and dying in this country, you'll see that we began with a kind of fatalistic materialism: "Well, it's in the cards." Originally, there was a religious tradition in this country positing that you go to heaven or you go to hell after death. Then, along came more and more materialism, and with it came a sense that death is the "end." Thus, because we see ourselves as our material identity, the intensive care unit keeps us alive at any cost, transplanting organs and we are trying to get the body to last longer and longer.

Next was Brother David Steindl-Rast, who holds degrees from the Vienna Academy of the Fine Arts and the Psychological Institute and who received his PhD in experimental psychology from the University of Vienna. He came to the United States with just a toothbrush and a copy of Martin Buber's *I and Thou* in his knapsack, before joining the newly-founded Benedictine monastery of Mount Saviour in Elmira, New York, where he received training in philosophy and theology.

Kramer: Brother David, let's begin with a creative question: What do you think is missing for most people with regard to their attitudes toward death and dying, the presence of which would transform their approach to death?

Br. David: I'll just tell you what comes to my mind off-hand. What's really missing is [being] fully alive. Because if we were fully alive right now, we wouldn't have to worry about being fully alive when it comes to dying and at that time we would know how to deal with it. You have to be very alive to deal with dying. It is something very active—the word "to die" in the English language, as in many other languages, has no passive voice. You can't say "I am being died." If you are "being died" you come out green or blue, but not dead. You can be killed and you will be killed sooner or later by something, but you have to die. That is something that you have to actively do. And so, if you really know how to live actively, you would also be able to die actively when life asks that from you.

If this particular interview becomes vital to you girls after I'm gone, could it be because what's missing for you now is the openhearted trust that in some unknown mysterious way I am still with you? (You can see the full interview on YouTube in several parts https://www.youtube.com/watch?v=UmuhWG-KvhI). My heart is always with you.

Bowing Deeply

My Respectful Beauties,

After several weeks of chilly, early morning June fog that would not burn off until early in the afternoon, if it did at all, this day began fully clothed in the sun. The air was cool and bright.

"Someone should take a picture of this," a club member said in the men's dressing room at the spa. "It's been a while since we've seen the sun this early."

I followed my usual routine. Carefully sitting, undressing, picking up my right leg with my good left arm and putting it back down, removing my jeans and shorts, then reversing the process by putting on my swimming suit, and aqua socks.

"It's all exercise, isn't it!" a middle-aged man dressing next to me observed. I smiled. "If you only knew," I said.

Pushing myself up from the bench and immediately grabbing the walker handles, I slowly move my way toward a row of sinks. Stopping at the first one, I run hot water over my earplugs before inserting them. Next, I hang my towel on a hook outside the shower to use later. Then, I plod my way—inch-by-inch—down the hallway, through the door, to the outside pool.

There, sitting on two lounge chairs, I see Meg, my Japanese friend and her American husband in their bathing suits.

"Where have you been? I haven't seen you for several weeks," I say. Meg usually swims at the same time every morning that I do.

"We just took some time off for ourselves," she responds.

"Oh, I thought that you might have been visiting your family in Japan."

"Not this time," she answers.

"Just yesterday," I mention, "I rediscovered a little booklet of haikus that I wrote while visiting Japan in the summer of '91, 'Unsent Postcards

III — Traveling West (1974-2000)

from Japan.'" Noticing that she was looking away, I leaned in closer. For reasons beyond my knowing, while standing with both hands clutching the walker, I began speaking animatedly.

"One hot afternoon in Tokyo, while sitting on a bench waiting for a bus, I looked across the street and saw an elderly man and an elderly woman speaking to one another. He was practically bald; her gray hair was pulled up in a bun. At one point, he bowed deeply to her; she, in turn, bowed deeply to him. He then bowed deeply to her; she, in turn, bowed deeply to him. After repeating this once again, he turned and walked away. She stood there quietly. Then, silently, she bowed again to the empty space in which he had stood. A silent dialogue had just happened."

Without any hesitation, Meg says, "That's a sign of respect. You don't find that in the younger generation anymore."

Quiet until now, her husband, who had been stretching out on his lounge chair carefully listening to the story, sits up: "Thank you for your pristine perception. The way you told it made me feel like I was right there!"

"Yes, I have often wished that I could have had a video camera to catch the magic of that event."

After swimming, I see them still sitting on their chairs. As I pass nearby, he says, "Thanks again for telling us your experience."

"You mean my pristine observation . . ."

"No, pristine perception," he insists. "It was like a category in the academy awards. What is that category? 'I was right there.'"

"I appreciate your appreciation," I say as I continue on back through the door to take a shower. How grateful I am for this walk-in shower's accessibility, for the grab bars, for the steaming hot water, for the silent dialogue taking place.

Here, my daughters, is a moment that I would not have experienced without MS. It forced me to sit still on that bench. It slows down the world's commotion for me. It allows me to focus on what's genuine, real, and most important. MS has given me gratefulness for the world which allows me to realize that I can bow deeply without moving.

Dialogic Awakening

My Sincere Leila and Yvonne,

Mechthild Gawlick—my closest, dearest, most genuine friend.

The year was 1995. In the fall, an inquisitive lady with short hair and a radiant smile came to my class. It was the German born Mechthild.

As you girls know, Mechthild is a woman who is not afraid to be wrong because she has no stake in being right. And she is not proud of what she has accomplished, which is no small amount. She, after all, raised three children in Germany and then in America.

Oh yes, and she cares for and supports family still living in Germany plus a growing number of friends in America. She is a woman who honestly would rather give, and give more, than receive. Being mildly disingenuous, as I often was, I recognize that one rarely meets such a genuine person. She is, I would discover, both open-minded and open-hearted, giving and forgiving.

The lady with the radiant smile who had a talent for listening was so intellectually curious that she talked to me after class many times. In our discussions, she recognized "something genuine" in me just beneath my various masks.

She had come into my class because she wanted to discuss dreams that she had in which a favorite Aunt in Germany was visiting her after dying. She shared stories with me of her childhood in Germany: of standing up against her lawyer father's anger; of running away and hiding from her parents; of giving her last money away to a friend in need; and of living within a fantastic dream-like imagination.

She spoke with an open heart, as if there was no agenda between us. She held nothing back and would not accept it when I did. We discussed Ultimacy. I was a practicing Catholic. She practiced the divinity of every moment. I said it was important to raise your children in a tradition, to give

III—Traveling West (1974–2000)

them something to rebel against. She said it was important to teach your children many traditions so that they can choose their own way.

One day, she brought a friend who was visiting from India to meet me in my office before class. They came. Fine, but I continued talking to another teacher who was there before them. She and her guest sat and waited until it was too late. It was time for the next class.

Our next conversation, and the one thereafter, came to a screeching halt. She asked me—face-to-face, eyes-to-eyes—for an apology before our dialogue could proceed.

I knew better than to say, as I had to others before, "That's just the way I am!" And I knew, in fact, that only honesty would be accepted.

When I was alone, I conjectured many rationalizations. I told myself, only half-heartedly, that I was ultimately right. It wasn't my fault. I had to do what I did in the way I did it. But none of these explanations would she accept. "We cannot go forward in our relationship," she insisted, "until we get through this bypass."

Stuck again.

Soon thereafter, we were discussing our roadblock. Sitting in my blue two-wheel drive Jeep before my "Death, Dying, and Religions" class, I said to her, "You have disappointed me." I could not let go of my overwhelming need to be right in this (and every) situation.

She responded, "No! You can be angry at me, you can be furious with me, but never disappointed because that means you expect me to match a fanciful image that is in your mind. I'll never be that." These words shook my hardheaded middle-aged brain. She was right, and I could only resolve the problem dialogically—person to person.

This came as a breakthrough insight that I knew to be true on arrival. Arising from the space between us, an invisible grace freed my ongoing resistance. Being mutual trumps being right!

I said to her, from a place deep inside, "I couldn't agree more." I reached across the space between us and hugged her, silently, deeply.

How did mom know?

While my mother was still alive in a nursing home with advanced dementia, Mechthild used to visit her before coming to visit with me. At times, we would visit my mother together. On one such occasion, while visiting Rose who was in one of her very alert moments, she looked up from her wheelchair into my eyes and said, "Don't let her get away because that would break my heart."

Dialogic Awakening

"Don't worry," I replied to my mother, "I won't!" And I haven't.

Mechthild remains my closest, dearest, most genuine dialogical partner. She is real and challenges me to keep it real.

It took this encounter with Mechthild, to wake me from the slumber of a deeply rooted ignorance. This is why I have deliberately used the term "awakening." It marks not only the shift from individualism to mutuality, but, even more importantly, from knowledge about dialogue to practicing it. Looking out, at last, through practicing eyes and really seeing/hearing the otherness of the other renews, for me, life's naked, unmediated splendor right here between us.

Dad's Death

My Independent Girls,

Yes, I was afraid of my father as I lived through my early years, but not to the point of failing to be proud of his virtues or to forgive his flaws. When I was a kid, he once (the only time that I can remember) took me to the 5th and Allegheny Rec. Center to fungo fly balls for me to chase and catch. His hands and arms were so large that he needed only one hand to swing the bat and launch fly balls toward the fence.

He taught me to drive defensively. "You'll never know what the other guy's going to do," he said. After I got my license, for my entire sixteenth year, he only let me drive the car with him. Four years later, he shocked me by handing me the keys to the family's new white '63 Ford Falcon to take myself, and my stuff, to theological school. For four years, this meant that my parents had to take trolleys or walk. Maybe he saw this as a pathway to my becoming a preacher.

And then, when he was sixty, he had a heart attack and was told to stop smoking. From the age of thirteen or so, he had smoked two packs of unfiltered Camels per day—two packs! When he heard the news, he never smoked another cigarette. And he never talked about it. I am proud of him.

I'm sure you remember, Yvonne, the evening that we visited grandpa when we thought he was about to die. We stood by his bedside in an intensive care unit. In those near death moments, he must have sensed the imminent danger. Suddenly, he looked up at me and said, haltingly, and with damp eyes: "I know I didn't always do a good job raising you. But I did the best I could." His wrinkled face looked weaker, softer and more approachable.

Without hesitation, and without seeking or needing a justification, I said: "I know you did, Dad. And you did a good job." He laid back and closed his eyes.

Dad's Death

When visiting hours were over, after we left, you asked me, "Dad, did you really mean what you said to your dad? You always told me that you didn't like him."

"I did, Yvonne," I responded, "and for at least two reasons. Just think if, for some reason, those were the last words that I had a chance to speak to my dad. I wanted them to be positive and loving. And second, given that my father never finished junior high school since he had to work to support his mother when his father died, and considering the severe limitations of the way in which he was raised, he really did do the best that he could."

Looking back over my shoulder years later, I now realize that what I said to my father at his bedside, and really meaning it, could only have happened in a moment of grace. My dad certainly was not the father of the year. He was an angry man, frustrated by the severe restrictions of his own upbringing. Like me, he was an only son. His anger, and, even worse, his heated outbursts at any moment, kept me living in constant fear. And worse, far worse, was his mental/psychological/emotional abuse of my mother, whom I loved and thought of as a saint.

Now, a call from the Nursing Home informing me that my father was nearing death brought you and me, Yvonne (Leila, you were in Michigan at the time) to his bedside. He was sitting up against the wall, just staring out into space like a blind person meditating. Across the hall, a gray-haired lady walked by, pushing her wheelchair ahead of her.

My words, "I love you dad. We love you," drew no response other than his blank stare.

Dad's skin was blue-grey. His speechless eyes stared at me. I looked at him as if I were looking at my own death about to happen. Still, there were no responses from my father.

"There is no way of knowing how soon it will be," a staffer in the Home told us. After a little while, it being a school-night, I told him again that I loved him and left.

At 10:45 am the next day (March 30th, 1995), he died. Even though his bed was too small, he got his money's worth for the month of March, which would have pleased him. Plus, I had the week off. "How did you know, Dad?"

He lived a simple life. He went away simply. No notice, without advertisement, without mourners, without words, he said goodbye.

III — Traveling West (1974–2000)

I wondered if he could feel the sting of what mom said when I told her (after she awoke in her wheelchair in her room): "He's dead mom. Dad . . . your husband . . . is dead!"

"It was predictable," she said, without any emotive charge.

I wondered if he knew before he died that each new attempt to speak about him would only backfire with more questions or leave me with empty words emerging from white spaces.

Did he know how proud I was when, at the recreation field with my friend, his huge right hand gripped the neck of my little league bat as he fungoed high-flys up and back into the early evening sky? With each swat of the ball, my dad stood taller in my eyes. Later, he stood even taller when he sold our Philadelphia house against my mother's will and bought the Quakertown property for $15,000, which later he sold for $107,000 before coming to California. Even though I speak more lovingly of my mother, my father is a far more interesting character.

And now I don't know what to say. This was my *father*. Where are my emotions? Buried under layers of selfish, fearful, dislike! "Don't leave me here," he once begged me when I returned him to the nursing home after taking him for a ride.

"I have to, dad!"

And I did, and it felt shitty to see him sitting helplessly in his wheelchair. Shitty. No one—dad included—should be left like that. I left wishing there was *something* I could do.

He was done with life, and it with him. "May it be easy for him," I prayed on into the night, "And may he continue to be able to fix things. And may he know how sorry I am that he didn't have the chances in life that I did. And that I wasn't the son that he wanted me to be. And may he know how grateful I am for the chances that I got largely because of him. And may he know that I forgive him, and love him and thank him."

And I forgive you, Dad, if there are/were things that you couldn't forgive about me.

So he leaves an enigma behind him. The man who infuriated me in my younger years, who psychologically and emotionally traumatized my mother—that person is a mystery to me. No, a mystery *in* me—in that part of myself that remains unavailable to me.

Yes, I want to get to know him. But I have zero ideas about who he was. Does he? How could I, unless I was able to write my father's story, which would turn up to be more fiction than fact. How crazy is that?

Dad's Death

Fourteen days after he died, he appeared to me in a dream (on Holy Thursday in the Christian calendar). The Roy Paul Kramer of guns, and books, and tools, and pictures, and supplies, and journals of gun data, who loved Milky Ways, in death, appeared in death, and this is how I recorded it in my dream journal:

I am in the kitchen dining room in my house eating breakfast. My father limps into the room. He is about to go to the hospital to have an operation on his leg.

"Are you all ready?" I ask.

"Yes," he says.

"Which leg is it?"

"My right leg."

He is wearing newly pressed, gray slacks. I can tell he is a bit tentative and wants some assurance. Without saying anything, he comes toward me and I extend my arms toward him, spontaneously and simultaneously.

I help him sit on my lap and I hug him close to me.

Nothing is said.

After a short while he stands, but instead of walking away, he turns and sits down again in my lap, this time facing in the other direction. At that moment, I kiss my father on the lips.

"You'll be alright, Dad," I say, "You're a tough old geezer."

Then I try to help him up, but his body is heavy and he doesn't seem to want to move.

"One, two, three, upzee!" I say and help him stand up.

And then I awoke, confused until further reflection convinced me that his gesture was one of forgiveness and that mine was one of reconciliation.

I wish I had embodied what the great playwright Chekhov once said: our talents come from our father, but our soul comes from our mother.

This is so spot on, it's scary.

Mom's Death

Dearest Sweethearts,

"She was too good for her own good," Mom's roommate, Rosie, screamed from the far side of the privacy curtain when she realized that mom had died. *Too good for her own good.* I begin with a memory of her sitting in her wooden rocking chair in Quakertown, with the dog my first wife gave her sitting on her lap, and then this brilliant memory turns to tears at the injustice of eighty-five years now ending.

Leave you must. Let go of my heart. Your last gift hurts. The living empathy you taught me for the other does not leave me.

I remember those moments when she didn't keep me to herself, and I gave her what freedom I could, and will now give her what will never leave her, give her away to others as she showed me how to give away myself.

After Church, often after the choir left, you waited for Frances. I watched, you listened. Walking home together, I asked, "Why?"

"She just needs someone to listen to her."

She never desired bangles, or beads, dresses, rings, or silver things. The gold she spun were the silent deeds spread across her days.

Dad is at the gun shop, and you, exhausted, are left to finish the housework by yourself, ironing dad's shirt, ironing my shirt and hanging it neatly alongside a new sports jacket that you bought earlier, and finally, ironing the same dress you wore last Easter and would again the next. This could not outdo you because you gave your entire self with what you gave.

When you died, the root soul of my life was swept away. When the morning came one more time to meet you and I found your eyes no longer open, the single Rose became the garden. Dried mouth open, lower lip bitten through, closed eyes — unmoving beauty. You belong to the Light now.

Somewhere she remembers, somewhere I remember. She never refused me. She always lifted me up. I always looked up to her. We prayed for one another. I continue to. In the midst of life's mile-for-mile, we climbed together. In the same kitchen where she washed and I dried, in the same kitchen where she taught me how to lace my shoes, she also taught me that "the mind is like a garden," and that Leos are astrologically "gregarious" and need to be the center of attention.

I don't let her go away into the day; I don't let her go away into the night. I intend to wait for her a long, long time. *I've been your only son, and your son only is what is behind my words.* I didn't learn love from books, and she never told me how to either, but I still learned it all from her.

Planning ahead, like always, let's meet in the Milky Way, Mom, to discuss what eyes have not seen and ears have not heard.

Because of the way things worked out, because I am still living in the home in which I raised my daughters, and because Leila and her husband Aaron live here and because they have a three-year-old daughter, Sienna Rose, and one-year-old son, Grayson Paul—your great grandchildren—all living here, you'd be happy to know that I'm keeping young. If only my body would cooperate!

And if there is a way for you to be aware of my feelings, please know that I'm not sure if I acted correctly at your death.

Leila and I immediately drove to her bedside on Saturday morning when the call came. She were unmoving. We were crying. I held her hand.

"I love you, Mom. I always will." Long moments pass.

Leila says, "I love you Grandmom."

III—Traveling West (1974–2000)

I massage her hand with my good hand. Her skin is wrinkled and bruised. Her fine white hair is still curly. My emotions are frozen high in my throat. There I am, modeling behavior that she modeled for me. There I am, not knowing what or how to best serve her. *Should I stay with you as you are dying or not?*

I ask because you always were—like my dad—a very private person.

When I was nine, my dad's mother was living with us. One Saturday, she fell after a stroke in an upstairs bedroom. Mom immediately gave me a dollar bill (which she didn't usually have) and sent me to the bowling lanes to spend the afternoon. When I returned, my grandmother was dead and had been taken to the mortuary. When I asked her why she had sent me away, my mom said: "I didn't want you to see her dead body!"

So Leila and I went home and waited. I hope I did the right thing.

Hours later, another call came. It was finished. On the afternoon of February 30th, 1998, Rose Tracey Kramer died at age eighty-five.

It was you, Mom, who taught me to pray. I pray that you are safe, that you are freed, that you can feel my limitless love for you reflected in your granddaughters.

An Anonymous Student

My Remarkable Daughters,

How amazing—my teaching career began and ended with a gift. It began in 1966 when a Yale student directed me to an open teaching position at his alma mater, Saint Andrews Presbyterian College in North Carolina. It ended—at least institutionally—when an anonymous student gave San Jose State University enough money to cover a full semester's salary for me so that I could begin writing a book on Martin Buber's *I and Thou*, which I then finished in retirement.

In 1999, just before retiring, I taught Buber's *I and Thou* for the first time to an upper division religious studies class. My attempt to get into the heart of the book—to choose its central themes, to illustrate them by quotation, interpretation, even diagrams, and to reference, along the way, Buber's other works that I believed made Buber's thought accessible to those who might otherwise find it impossible to grasp—largely failed.

As I recall, the text was too difficult for most students to apprehend. There were two German-speaking students who did find it understandable, and a middle-aged woman who would write a paper on how Buber's I-Thou dialogue helped her relate to her autistic son. How surprised I was, therefore, when I received a call from the dean's office. What? Why?

Sitting with the dean in her office the next day, she said, "I have some good news for you."

"What is it?" I responded, completely clueless as to what she might say.

Smiling straight ahead, she said, "You're not going to believe this, but a student who has been in several of your classes and who wishes to remain anonymous has come to me and offered the University $150,000. $100,000 is to be used to pay your salary for an entire semester along with clerical assistance so that you can begin to write the book that you are eager to write

III — Traveling West (1974-2000)

on Martin Buber. $50,000 of the gift was to be given to the Religious Studies Program. What do ya think?"

What do you think, I thought? "I'm . . . I'm amazed! I'm ecstatic! I'm thrilled! Are you sure?" I almost leapt out of my seat.

Somehow, the San Jose Mercury News picked up the story and, from there, it spread across the country. As a result, I received a letter from a woman in Texas named Phyllis A. Anderson, who told me of once meeting Buber in his home. Her account of that experience was so compelling that I included it in the book, *Martin Buber's I and Thou: Practicing Living Dialogue*:

> In 1963 I had a grant to study in Israel for six weeks. I traveled there with a group directed by Professor Menahem Mansoor—at that time head of the Department of Hebrew and Semitic Studies, University of Wisconsin, Madison.
>
> Dr. Mansoor was well known in Israel and we were invited to have tea and a short meeting with Martin Buber at his home in Jerusalem. It was hot but the stone house had tiled floors, high ceilings, and window blinds that let the breeze through, but moderated the sunlight. Every room was lined, ceiling to floor, with books and large library ladders on rollers, even the dining room. There was a very young child playing with a kitty. After tea we stood around the dining room and in came a frail, fragile looking old man in house shoes. The child crawled into his lap and he spoke briefly, then told us we could ask questions. We were all awed by the situation but there were questions. Finally, he indicated that he was tired, so only one more question. Someone asked, "Dr. Buber who do you think has been the greatest man in history?" Buber paused a moment, almost as if surprised and said quietly: "Why, there are *no* great men, only useful ones." Then he rose, smiled a gentle smile, bowed slightly, and shuffled out to the kitchen where women were preparing a meal. Our group exited in total silence.

If you read this report carefully, you can see why Buber is a rare teacher. He lived what he taught. He himself is not *great* but *useful*. Here is a remarkable verbal account of an eighty-three year old, world-renowned scholar/writer serving tea and teachings to strangers in his home.

Girls, I know that you've heard me speak often of all that I've learned from Buber's teaching. I have probably talked about it too much. But please know that not only has it made me a better person, but it has specifically made me a better father. I bow to this man with a child on his lap.

Why? I can't tell you how many times he has made me catch myself, and turn toward you each to pay deeper attention to what you are saying, thinking, and experiencing. Sure, I learned the basics of the art of dialogue from your grandmom. Sure, I knew that the key to conversation was listening. Sure, I brought what grandmom had shown me into our relationship.

However, because of my intellectual grounding, the philosophical basis that Buber lays out for the life of dialogue (turning, addressing, listening, and responding) guides me, more skillfully than another person or author I've encountered.

But how does practicing Buber's dialogical thought make me feel? Released! I am released from thinking that I know, by myself, what to do. Genuine dialogue feels liberating because it occurs not in me, but in our interactions in the Between. When we are deeply exchanging raw, emotive ideas, I can look suddenly out the window and see that the sun has set—that hours have passed, and that, though fully present, I have lost all track of time and place. I know you girls know what I'm talking about and how mutually liberating it feels.

IV

Retiring
(2000– . . .)

Retirements

Dear Leila and Yvonne,

I began the new millennium with two retirements—the first from twenty-five years of teaching at San Jose State University, the second, shortly thereafter, from twenty-five years of Roman Catholic practice.

Just before retiring my neurological assessment read:

> Kenneth Kramer, Professor of Comparative Religious Studies at San José State University, was diagnosed with Multiple Sclerosis at the age of twenty-six (1967) when he was discovered to have retrobulbar optic neuritis. In Kenneth's case, the disease has taken the relapsing-remitting form, which over the years has degenerated his physical abilities causing the following symptoms: dizziness and lack of balance; right side drop-foot; severely diminished use of his right arm; lack of energy; difficulty walking unaided (even with a cane); difficulty dressing self; difficulty accomplishing any two-handed task; the need to wear an AFO orthotic; and a weakened bladder.

My father was able to retire early from driving a truck, and I was able to retire early from teaching. His reason was a heart attack; mine, MS. And so I retired at sixty, which I would never have done had I not been given the gift of MS. I say "gift" here because it has given me the chance to look back at my life, a chance to relax, to regroup, and to push ahead all the more vigorously with writing projects I'd already begun or imagined.

At first, I missed the creative interactions I'd always had with students and colleagues in classrooms, in hallways, in office hours—any place I met students. How great it is when a student finds comfort and direction from educational insights shared in the classroom and beyond. I don't, however, miss the endless committee meetings, restrictive new regulations, and lack of educational funding.

IV—Retiring (2000– . . .)

But, to this day, I have not lost my desire and willingness to teach, whether at my house or, when invited, at the University. In that sense, I never actually retired from teaching, nor do I ever expect to.

When I say that I retired, or graduated, from Catholicism, I mean that it was a fairly easy shift from attending Sunday Mass to no longer following liturgical Catholicism at all. How does one retire from Catholicism?

For me, it involved a confluence of the increasing diminishment of my physical body along with a gradually decreasing respect for the church. When you let go and nothing holds you back, you graduate.

When I realized the transcendent currents that flow through the church also flows through every sacramental event/encounter/awakening, my spirituality was not lost or diminished, but deepened and refreshed. "So instead of getting to heaven at last," as Emily Dickinson once wrote, "I'm going all along."

Yes, I missed choral worship, communal prayer, and provocative homilies. How great it is, though, when the worshipper's dark nights are liberated into spiritual light.

Just as my words about retiring from twenty-five years of teaching are short and to the point, my explanation about retiring from Catholicism is all too brief. I would need to write a book on that alone to begin explaining reasons for my disassociating from a 2000 year old institution.

It could be said, in fact, that I haven't abandoned the Church at all, but that, rather, we had an amicable parting of ways. The discovery of the Eucharistic presence of God throughout the world allowed me to recognize the truth of what Buber called "Sacramental Existence."

So it was without thought, without plan, that the next day after meeting with the Dean, I picked up my pen (now with my left hand) and continued working on my first Martin Buber book. It was Buber who once said, "To be old is a glorious thing, when one has not unlearned what it means to begin."

What a way to begin my new life.

Risking Enchantment

My Proud Daughters,

At my retirement dinner, initiated by the Religious Studies faculty, unbeknownst to me, my former student, Todd Perreira, took it upon himself to construct a booklet of testimonials in my honor. He gathered several paragraph-long affirmations from then-current faculty and students, and from my good friends Mishael Caspi and Maurice Friedman. It had been over a year since I had last taught. In the meantime, I'd started using a cane to assist me.

The booklet began with what my former coordinator in Religious Studies, Benton White called "Funny, perhaps eccentric letters that he received from someone whom he assumed to be an aspiring poet, or a leftover hippy." Benton went on to say, "One of the smarter things I did in my college career was to hire you."

Maurice Friedman wrote, "This is the time for me to bear witness . . . To me, Kenneth Kramer is both saint and suffering servant . . . a pure spirit unsullied by time . . . "

Chris Jochim, who became coordinator of Religious Studies years after we were each hired, wrote, "Ken has been a lesson in optimism, one who understands the joy of life."

Richard Keady, my colleague over the years, wrote, "You have been at the center of developing our program's identity, and shaping its place in the university."

Another colleague, Jennifer Rycenga shared, "Kramer's mind always smiles through his eyes. The eyes hold a light of celebration along with the laughter of celebration."

Brent Walters, a former student and then a colleague, writes "As a scholar, you permitted the text to speak for itself without compromising its message and led us through a wilderness of challenges. . . ."

IV—Retiring (2000– . . .)

Mishael Caspi wrote, "He became what my teacher Martin Buber was—the one who led me to the window and pointed out to what he sees awaiting for my response."

Mechthild, my dear friend who graciously provided her dining room for the retirement meal which she also cooked, wrote, "Genuine dialogue came alive between us and we carry it together to deeper and deeper levels."

Todd ended these testimonials with his own: "By empowering students to become their own teachers, by inviting the material to address the student in their particularity, he can give himself wholly and unconditionally without ever exhausting or withholding his gifts from anyone."

Not without some risk, I include these selected sentences from my colleagues who knew me well, who worked with me, and who completely embarrassed me with their genuine and sweet words. When I read them, I turn red. I'm still not sure if I should have included these testimonies here.

Knowing you girls as I do, I think they belong.

A Large Cup of Java

Dearest Yvonne,

During the years that I drank my single cup of coffee at 3pm each day, you and I shared the hour together on days when you were able to drop by. Right around 3 o'clock in the afternoon, you would come to the house to make me a large cup of java.

I will never forget those picturesque moments and the serious precision with which you would grind the organic, fresh coffee beans, which always reminded me of the Zen ritual of tea. Then, you would place the ground coffee into a French press and, carefully, pour heated water over the crushed beans.

Your long, wavy blonde hair seemed to catch the sunlight. You would be illuminated—gracefully moving about the kitchen. You were always full of new stories as delicious in your life as the smell of the freshly brewing coffee, almost as if it was your story making my java.

We would then proceed, with you drinking your green tea, to discuss whatever issues were up for you—usually involving young men. At times, however, you would be interested in seeking out my advice about one of your friend's life-dramas.

I remember saying to you on one afternoon, "Hey Yvonne," looking directly into your sparkling green eyes, "how much do I love you? More than all the coffee in the world."

And you know how I love my coffee.

Sacramental Existence

My Inquisitive Daughters,

Mechthild—who helped me become true to myself simply by being herself, whose certitude always arose in response to the demands of each unique situation, whose dialogue drew forth what was most genuine, and who, like my mother, gave where the need was greatest, and then gave more—had prepared three plates of tangerine slices and made green tea.

As Fr. Mark Stetz (a former disc jockey and news reporter who was then in his fifteenth year of priesthood) arrived, Mechthild and I were discussing her recent experiences in Japan and Korea. Fr. Mark was a tall, sturdy, handsome priest who delivered up-to-date homilies.

"There," Mechthild said after we all sat at the table, popping a tangerine slice in her mouth, "the sacred is brought into everyday life through ritual enactments; in the Christian Church the sacred is relegated to worship on Sundays. There's an unfortunate split between what happens during one hour on Sunday and the rest of the week."

"Even though I am a priest in a highly ritualistic tradition," Fr. Mark said, joining in, "I don't appreciate too much ritual. Actually," he said, "I wasn't raised Catholic. I was raised in the Ukrainian tradition, where there is an excess of ritual. And because I didn't understand the language, much of its significance escaped me."

"By ritual," Mechthild said, "I simply mean inviting moments of the sacred into life. Ritual means, for me, that every moment is sacred activity into which we live."

Since Fr. Mark had just come from a funeral service, our conversation naturally shifted to questions of death and the afterlife. At one point, he said, "It's remarkable to think that the deceased person who is being mourned by his family is now in the kingdom of God's unconditional love.

Sacramental Existence

Just imagine what that must be like to be in the presence of such a great love."

"Though I can't even begin to imagine it," I said, "when I do, I sometimes wonder about the possibility of growing or changing or discovering in that situation."

"But Ken," Mark replied, "remember there's no time in the afterlife."

"Yes, and that's why it's so difficult to imagine what will occur."

"Yes and no," Mark said. "We do, however, have brief moments in this world in which we slip into timelessness and forget time."

"That's one of the things Buber says happens when people enter into a genuine dialogue," Mechthild added. "They lose track of time and, only after finishing the dialogue, realize how much time has passed."

"That's a good segue," I said, "for the emerging recognition of the 'cosmic Eucharist' as two-fold."

This concept of the two-fold "cosmic Eucharist" emerges from an interaction between contemplative Christian monasticism and eighteenth-century Hasidic Judaism. In fact, the initial distinction that triggered my thinking about this spiritual sensibility was made by a Benedictine priest, Fr. Bruno, who wrote that there is a difference between *two sacramental visions*: ecclesial and cosmic. By *ecclesial*, he meant the divine presence that flows through the sacraments of baptism and Eucharist, and by cosmic he was referring to the divine presence that flows through the entire created world.

"Yes," he replied, "you mentioned that to me on the phone awhile back."

"Yes, and it makes even more sense when you apply the Hasidic Jewish understanding of sacramental existence to what Fr. Bruno means by cosmic sacramentality. That is, in every genuine relationship between persons, or with whatever is in your presence (e.g., nature or art), the love, mercy, and justice of the divine presence pours through the heart of the interrelationship. This is the covenantal God whose promise to Moses at Sinai is to be present as the one who is present, and to Abraham and the prophets, to be a reliable dialogical partner."

At this point, Mechthild said, "That's why Buber's translation of what God says to Moses in Exodus 3 is '*Ich bin da*.' *Da* means 'here', or 'there', or, better yet 'fully present.'"

"That makes such a difference," I said, "from the way it is usually translated ('I am that I am'). Consider, what happens when you enter into

IV—Retiring (2000– . . .)

an open-minded, open-hearted relationship with another person who surrenders, as you do, into what Buber calls the 'sacrament of dialogue.' For instance, juxtapose how Thomas Merton characterizes the cosmic aspect of the Eucharistic sacrifice ('elevation,' 'consecration,' and 'transformation') with what Martin Buber writes about 'sacramental existence' (turning towards the fullness of life, hallowing every-day relationships, and becoming reciprocally transformed)."

In the pause that ensued, Mark's face revealed his hesitation. "Our language is so insufficient at this point," he said. "I understand what Buber is saying and accept much of it. For instance, I have participated in a dialogue in which there were layers of awareness and people were completing each other's thoughts and taking off from different levels but always returning to the subject at hand, to the common thread of the conversation."

When it came to a completion, and we all sat back in a peaceful relaxation, I could only come to describe what had happened as a real encounter where each person was able to be completely at peace with the others. However, Mark resisted the notion of God's redemption occurring.

"Mark," I said, "I hope you didn't hear me speak of God's being redeemed. Buber never speaks that way. On the other hand, he speaks of genuine dialogue's revealing God's redemptive presence."

At that point, I went into the other room to find a book by Buber that I wanted to give to Fr. Mark, and he and Mechthild, meanwhile, continued their conversation about the Eucharistic presence in everyday life. When I returned, Fr. Mark indicated that he needed to leave. Unnoticed by the three of us, several hours had passed.

"I brought the consecrated host," he said. "Do you want it?"

I shook my head, indicating that I didn't think it was necessary.

"I didn't think so," Mark said, nodding to the dining table, "because we've had the Eucharist already."

After Fr. Mark left, we continued sitting at the sun-bathed table, sipping green tea. Referring to a conversation we once had shortly after meeting each other (when I had spoken of the Catholic Church more admiringly), Mechthild said, "Kenneth Paul, see . . . you *are* the learning kind." She spoke with a sunny-brightness that radiated from her eyes.

"Wait a minute," I said, putting my cup of tea down on the wooden table. Directing my undivided attention to her, I said, "And so are you! That's one of the reasons I like you so much."

"For me," she said, "it's that. But it's also because we are each other's teachers."

"You couldn't be more right," I affirmed. "Ever since our early conversations about dialogue itself and about texts, our children and grandchildren, about German language and culture, and especially about what makes relationships genuine, we have been each other's teacher."

At that point, she refilled our now empty teacups.

"That's why I told Friedman," I said as she was filling her cup, "it was Mechthild. He had asked me, 'What brought you back to Buber?' Immediately I told him about that breakthrough dialogue we had before class at SJSU—a dialogic awakening, a new relationship between us."

Although you girls may not see the significance of this event, I tell this episode here because it allows me to return to your original question—"Dad, since you've studied so many different religions and spiritual practices, what about your own journey?" Although Father Mark did not/could not fully agree with us (and Buber) about the redemptive significance of sacramental existence, he knew he never needed to contact me again.

And he didn't.

So, if I am no longer Baptist, no longer Buddhist, and no longer Catholic, what am I? Buber once reluctantly responded to that analogous question with the phrase "a believing humanist," by which he meant a human being who trusts in the reciprocity between humanity and the "eternal Thou." I know what he means by this phrase, but it doesn't quite work for me. Actually, no phrase does. So I guess it's better to say that I'm living spiritually without being religious, bowing deeply to an eternal Other, in whom I fully trust.

Still Swimming at Sixty-Five

My Inspiring Beauties,

Now at age sixty-five, I realize how blessed I am (beyond any reasonable person's expectations) to have maintained a creatively curious mind, a vital voice, and communities of interested and interesting friends. It's true that my MS has affected my mobility and my balance, taking away portions of each gradually. It's also true that every movement of my body is affected. I still "walk" only because I am aided by my four-wheel walker. Now, I need assistance with almost everything, although I can still use the toilet and get dressed, but these abilities are disappearing, too.

As a writer, thinker, and promulgist, I like to pay strict attention to the ever-new, surprising interactions between people whom I meet in my limited appearances in the world. Now, I rarely have this option. My entire right side has been compromised. From a central schitoma in my right eye to the inability to lift my right arm, hold things, write, comb, brush, tie, zip, wipe, shake, and stir, to a drag-leg and a drop-foot (which I used to be able to pull off).

Watching my mother navigate her way through the Nursing Home before she died, with an institutional walker that had cut tennis balls on the front legs so that it would slide easier along the polished floor, I never thought that I'd be this glad to obtain and maintain a deluxe, light-weight, collapsible, four-wheel mobilizer with hand brakes, a seat, and a basket. Now, I can no longer walk without it. I move like an inchworm, dragging one leg one step at a time.

Since MS has (after all these years) finally made its presence painfully obvious, it's impossible for me to continue hiding out. One day, as I was entering the local health club where I went to swim, a seventy-something young woman approached me, as if she'd been waiting for this opportunity to engage me in conversation. Not out of the blue (but I no longer recall the context), she spoke about not being afraid to die and about "hardly being able to wait to find out what happens."

"Fascinating," I responded. "I was just thinking that each time I jump into the swimming pool and the medium in which I exist changes instantaneously from air to water, it feels like dying. I wonder if that's what it will be like at death." I spoke about the Jewish tradition's insistence on choosing life over death, and she responded that it was very difficult for her not knowing what will happen at death. But I said, "If you find out now, then there will be no surprise."

"The surprise," she grinned, "will come in the details."

I include this letter to you girls because of the bare encounter between two elderly people in a surprising moment of time "between the lines of age." Even though we were total strangers, we shared words that lifted and renewed each other.

Twin Lakes Prayers

Beachfront Daughters,

Each day after swimming, I'd leave the health club at about 10:45 a.m. for an 11 o'clock date with silence—no phone, no watch, no radio, no sounds beyond occasional seagulls, waves crashing on the beach, and conscious and unselfconscious breathing.

I turn, turn away from the road, from the riddles of daily life, toward where steps lead down to the beach. Once a day, at the same time each day, at the same place between the East and West side of Santa Cruz, between the land and the sea, between swimming and writing, I turn to contemplative prayer, to deep listening.

Father, thank You; Father, thank You; Father, thank You. I synchronize "Fath-" with inhaling and "—ther" with exhaling. I synchronize "thank" with inhaling and "You" with exhaling. Fath-ther. Thank You. Fath-ther. Thank You. Fath-ther. Thank You.

Until emptiness.

Each time self-consciousness returns, "Fath-ther. Thank You" just continues.

I sit in the car seat of my Jeep, my arms supported by the door handle and the console between front seats. No longer institutionally religious, mixing spiritual practices that I've learned along the way, I sit, eyes closed, rhythmically breathing.

Settling; settling; settling. Letting go. Listening; listening; hearing. Bowing to emptiness. The alone with the Alone.

For years (until I could no longer drive), I was alone like this every day at the earth's edge—praying to the Eternal Listener; listening to the Eternal Responder. Each day, breathing in this contemplative way; each day, praying in this spontaneously disciplined way.

Twin Lakes Prayers

This is not what I've been taught to do, and not how I've been shown to do it, but when I listen meditatively, I hear words like:

> Infuse me with Your invisible grace, Father, thank You
> for setting my body/mind/heart on You, in You, through You,
> thank You for surrendering my will to Yours,
> for contentment with my afflictions, Father,
> for earthly Angels who help us in unexpected ways,
> thank You for little by little by little casting off distractions . . .
> please direct me as I write to say what You would have me say.

Every time I came to Twin Lakes beach, I knew that I was not alone. I hope that anytime you come here, you feel the same certainty, knowing that in the lightness of being I'll be there with you, still listening and still praying.

Tuesdays with Todd

Wonder-filled Ladies,

Todd once asked me to write a short autobiography. When I asked him to be more specific, he responded, "That's easy: it's your relationship to MS. MS is a game changer and you know it. It's the 'wife' who never left you. It's the 'gift' you never asked for. I think that must be the lens through which your entire memoir should be written and read. Your narrative has to be grounded in the brokenness of your body."

It was a chilly, sunny, early December Tuesday as Leo, my thirty-one year old caregiver, wheeled me into Todd's "Death, Dying and Religions" class. Todd had asked me to come and address Buber's dialogical view of death. Once inside, Leo helped me out of the red transport chair and into the teaching chair behind the desk. I asked him to move me to the side of the desk instead so that there would be nothing between the students and me.

When Leo first met me, seeing the many books on religion that surrounded me, he asked, "What is your religion?" Smiling, yet seriously, I answered, "I was born a Baptist, I became a Buddhist and then a Catholic, but now I'm living religiously, without being religious. Or, better put, I am a quirky herminute (as Todd once described me) who has journeyed from being religious to living dialogically."

While Todd was returning papers to some of the class members, I quickly asked several students in the front row, "Who would feel comfortable reading something to the class for me? Who wants to read a paragraph about Todd from my book?" A girl with short cut, light hair hurdled her initial hesitation and designated herself as "the reader." Quicker than a handful of other students could respond to my softly asked question, I gave her a copy of my new book *Learning Through Dialogue* and showed her a paragraph I wanted her to read after we started. It was our secret.

I turned to Todd and said, "Let me first acknowledge you as the special teacher that you are." And then turning to face the class, I said, "I have taken the liberty to bring Todd a gift from all of us."

At this point, I nodded to another student, to whom I had given a large envelope that contained a copy of *Learning through Dialogue* inscribed, as I told the class, "From your students in the 2013 DDR class, along with today's provocateur in recognition of your special teaching abilities."

The student who had agreed to read a paragraph from the preface of the book then took over:

> It was in my "Death, Dying and Religions" class at San José State University that I first met Todd Perreira. My earliest memory of Todd was his extraordinary thoroughness and remarkable competence in completing class work. He was one of the few students I've taught who actually wanted to read more than what was assigned. His enthusiasm for learning initiated a relationship of trust or what Maurice Friedman calls "existential grace."

"Oh," I interjected a smile, "But Todd's supposed to introduce me."

The students laughed and turned their attention to him. He sat in the front of the room off to the side of the class wearing a cream colored suit which highlighted his dark bow tie.

Speaking more slowly than usual, he talked directly and clearly about why he took every class that I offered.

"When you find a good teacher, the subject no longer matters. It's the teaching. Doctor Kramer, as you will see, is that kind of teacher. He once met with me and two friends weekly over the summer to direct us through a deep reading of the *Bhagavad Gita* to help us understand one of Eliot's main sources in his *Four Quartets*."

After speaking convincingly of the impact that Martin Buber's dialogical philosophy has had on him, he turned his attention to the class at hand and said, "We want you to bring your questions into a dialogue."

"Yes," I added, looking around the entire room. "I want to hear where you are at this point in the semester." I waited silently for what might be said.

A student in the front row cautiously raised her hand. "Do you belong to any religion?" she asked. I felt as if I had been thrown a beach ball to catch.

"Briefly," I said, "very briefly—because this could eventuate into a long answer: I was born and raised a conservative Philadelphia Baptist, the kind

IV—Retiring (2000– ...)

that didn't believe in dancing and did believe that Jesus walked on water. By the time I reached grad school, I was completely absorbed by Zen Buddhism and was for the next few years a Buddhist. When it became clear to me that my Buddhism was more in my mind than in my entire life, and after I met three penguins dressed as Benedictine Monks, and after spending countless hours discussing theological and ecclesiastical issues with them, along with meeting and reading other Benedictine monks, I was received into the Roman Catholic Church.

"For the next twenty-five years, I attended Mass without fail. Mind you, I wasn't your typical parish Catholic. Oh no, I was one of those mystical contemplative types. It was a wonderfully necessary place for me to be in my mid-life, but after engaging Martin Buber's way of dialogue and being engaged by eighteenth century, everyday, Hasidic holiness, I've retired from being religious. Now, I believe dialogically.

"Now, I live in trust what has been given to me. I trust that the Holy Other is present in and through every genuine dialogue both inspiring my words for others and theirs for me. It is remarkable every time that it happens."

The class went quiet; all the students had fixed their attention on me. I sat in my jeans and a long-sleeved pullover collared beige shirt. A young man of just a few words raised his hand. He asked—very succinctly, very directly, a five-word question: "What is your greatest fear?" Between his speaking it and my hearing it arose a reminder not to make an unthinking response.

"That's difficult for me," I respond, looking at the student. "I fear dying in a puddle of pain such that I can't access trust and gratitude, such that all my energy is pain-drained."

A silence followed.

After more discussion, when I ask,—"Is there anything else?" Todd said, "Let me connect some of the dots. I know you have studied the world religions and have written a book on them. I know you have gone to India, Jerusalem, and Japan. I know you have become a Buddhist and a Catholic and that now you are something different. I also know that you have MS and that it has greatly diminished your physical abilities. What role has MS played in your faith stance?"

"MS has given me a spiritual practice, an everyday, all-the-time presence, combined with prayer. Why? Because MS is with me every moment of every day. There is no escaping it. Every day, I am offered a choice: either accept and make the most of it or resist and try to deny it. MS's ever-increasing degeneration of my motor skills forces me to slow down. I was always—still am in spurts—over amped. The gift of 'Em-effin-S' as my friend with MS in Philadelphia calls it, is that it plays a game of takeaway.

"When I could no longer deny, dismiss, or divorce myself from its effects, when I had to give in, I slowed down, and when I did, the world showed up differently. What I had failed to notice about people became noticeable. Genuineness separated itself loudly from disgenuineness. MS became the Buddha saying: 'a person who is concentrated [gathered together at the center] knows a thing as it really is.'"

After class, a girl with long brunette hair clasping her hands in front of her approached me timidly.

"Thank you for coming," she said, reaching out to take my extended left hand. I detected some disturbance behind her smile as I said, "You're welcome."

"I enjoyed hearing that you raised your daughters." In response to a question, "Do you have children?" I had explained that I raised you girls from the ages of six and eight as a single parent and that we have become so close that I often tell you both that "we raised each other."

"I wish I had a father like you," she said, wiping her eyes.

IV—Retiring (2000-...)

Gingerly, I touched her arm and asked about her parents. Her emotional state prevented an immediate response. Tears replaced words. I waited quietly.

Wiping her eyes some more, she said, "My father was an alcoholic and finally left." She continued wiping away her tears.

"And your mom?" I said. "What about your mom?"

"Yes, I have a good mom."

"Oh, see, it's as I've always told my girls—as long as you have one parent who loves you unconditionally you can make it!"

"I just want to thank you," she said, "for loving your daughters the way you did." I hugged her with one arm and she left.

And I just want to thank you, girls, for loving me the way you do.

Ever-Narrowing Confines

My Healing Daughters,

Girls, have you ever been as frightened, as scared for me as I have been at times for you?

I ask you because I realize that I've tried to stay in the closet (with MS) as long as I could, until a cane made it obvious.

You know I've lived in denial by remaining close to home, by communicating over the phone, throughout my teaching and writing career, and face-to-face with you—the plural you—my closest friends, in and through all of my denial, in and through all of my fears.

Now, in my seventy-first year, for the first time in my life, I broke a bone: the humerus in my right arm. As a result of the fracture, I was introduced to the world of adult diapers, and needing assistance getting from my motorized wheelchair onto the toilet. During the six-week recovery period—which, I must confess, I didn't think would ever end—I received a "bed bath" each morning before sitting in my motorized chair. Each day was punctuated with visits from health planners, nurses, my typist, and phone calls from well-wishers. Each day, I was thrown back upon myself and made to peer deeply within to examine what resources were still available to enable me to help me pass through this situation.

Shortly after this six-week hiatus, during which I missed my routine visits to the spa, I fell again and fractured the tibia and fibula in my right leg.

It happened on a Friday afternoon in my bathroom as I was turning to back my way onto the toilet, as I have done so many times. Suddenly, for reasons unknown to me, my right leg simply gave way. I came down. Whereas I was still able to use my legs to an extent before that happened, now I need assistants to help me transfer from bed to chair, from chair to toilet, from chair to bed—to lift up my body, to hold up my leg. Think of all

IV—Retiring (2000– . . .)

the motor skills I'm losing that I will need to revitalize when these bones are re-cemented.

Rather than anger (at whom should I be angry . . . myself?), my overwhelming immediate response was depression. At seventy-one, I was told that I would, from that point forward, have to spend all of my time in a wheelchair. This meant that I could no longer drive for myself.

Wait a minute! My freedom of movement—both in the house and outside—was suddenly removed. I had to stop driving, which I had done for fifty-five years (from sixteen to seventy-one). That was it! From one day to the next, a total life-change. I thought of what Jack Benny once said when he was receiving a comedy award: "I don't really deserve this award, but I have arthritis, and I don't deserve that either." The thought that all life is a gift, that this moment's inhalation and exhalation is a remarkable lesson, wasn't enough to override the sadness, anxiety, fear, or apprehension. Now what!?

The next day, sitting in my motorized wheelchair in the back of a handicapped accessible taxicab, on the way to the doctor's office, I had a remarkable conversation with a well-read yet somewhat eccentric cab driver. It turned out that he was someone who had spent a lot of time studying history, especially, as he told me, the history of the American Civil War.

All I could see of this man was his scruffy cheeks and dark-brown eyes in the rearview mirror, darting around at the road. "What do you think caused the Civil War?" I asked him after a moment of silence.

"It definitely came down to economic reasons," he replied without hesitation. "When the institution of slavery was threatened, the southern states recognized the financial difficulties that would follow if slavery were eliminated." Another moment of silence.

"I asked you that question because a professor (Richard DeMartino), once told of beginning his career as a student of history, especially of the Civil War. Yet when he tried to answer the question of what caused the Civil War, he wound up in Zen Buddhism. That is, the real cause of the Civil War was the human condition—its duplicitous, internally unresolved nature."

"Of course," the cab driver, said, shooting a glance at me in the mirror, "the human condition lies underneath everything we do." His sunglasses sat on top of his head throughout the conversation, without ever moving. The directness, the sharpness, the certitude of his speaking reminded me, ever so slightly, of DeMartino.

Then he added, "I've been living with two questions recently. The first is, how can I turn a negative into a positive? The second is, how can I turn a positive into a more positive?"

"Those questions, especially the first, are of interest to me not in the generic sense, but with regard to my particular situation right now," I replied. "Let me ask you a question. How can I turn my negative situation of a broken leg into a positive one?"

"Oh," he said, "that's a question which only you can answer for yourself. You have to live with that one."

Since then, I have been doing just that. And one way of doing just that is to ask friends and family members who are intimately and immediately interested in my situation for any suggestions they might have. No answers, however, emerged over the first week-and-a-half of my wheel-bound life that gave me any direction. I had no answer when people asked me if, when they saw me subsequently, I had arrived at anything. Up until yesterday, it didn't seem to me that anything was going to show up, either.

But the night before yesterday, I had a dream. I was with my long-deceased father, who had smoked two packs of Camel cigarettes every day up until his heart attack at age sixty, when he stopped smoking cold turkey. In the dream, he had half an unlit cigarette hanging from his mouth that he was trying to light so that he could finish smoking it. There was a little bit of empty space between the tobacco inside the paper and the paper surrounding it at the tip. I took the cigarette and crimped it, found a match, dragged the match against the striker until it ignited, put the cigarette in my mouth, and lit it. I thought I might as well take a few puffs and get a little buzz before I gave it to him, which I then did. He took pleasure in finishing the cigarette.

The next day, I received a visit from my very real dialogical partner, Mechthild. She presented me with her homemade persimmons cookies and I presented her with an inscribed copy of my latest book, *Martin Buber's Spirituality: Hasidic Wisdom for Everyday Life*, which is dedicated to her. First, she read the inscription and hugged me tightly. Then she read the epigraph and said, "I can see why you selected this as the book's epigraph." Then she read the dedication: *For Mechthild Gawlick, who turns to engage me unreservedly on the "narrow ridge" of genuine dialogue.* She paused. She looked into my eyes. She reached over and hugged me and squeezed me tightly.

"You didn't have to do this," she said.

IV—Retiring (2000–...)

"There was never a doubt," I responded.

In the course of our subsequent conversation, I told her of my dream the night before. "What do you think it is saying to me?" I asked her.

"I think it's a healing dream," she responded. Over the years, we had traded our dreams with each other, offering suggestions on their potential meanings. She not only knew my life circumstances very well, but she also knew of the difficult relationship I had with my father while he was alive.

"In what way is it a healing dream?" I asked.

"Well," Mechthild began, "not only did you offer to and actually help your father to do something that he very much enjoyed, but you also participated with him by doing it yourself. He knew you didn't smoke. He knew you didn't like cigarettes. This act probably pleased him very much, that you would join him in doing something that he so enjoyed. I think that your smoking with him brought you a little closer to him."

Consider, girls, how and why this story begins—with me feeling wrath and depression from my MS-caused broken leg, and ends—with me having a dream in which I want to heal my father. Not myself, but him.

What do you think the connection is between the two? I'd really like to know.

The Turn Not Taken

Dear Leila,

Bed, bath, done.

Dressed for the day; set in my chair; happy voices pull me left, not right.

I leave the bedroom and head toward the dining room, not toward my den and the morning newspaper, but toward you, my son-in-law, and grandkids.

Aaron's cooking eggs for Mama, Sienna's eating cereal, and Mama's holding Grayson.

I roll up behind Sienna and rub her back.

"I'm here: I love you".

"Sienna," Papa calls from the kitchen, "wanna go surfin'?"

"I want bread," she yells, gets down from her seat, comes to my chair, stands on my feet, and resting on the pedals, tries to climb up into my empty lap.

I grab her jammies and pull.

Together, we achieve lift off; she turns and faces the table—

There we are.

"Dad," you say, your hazel green eyes gazing directly into mine, "you look good, full of life." Your smile fills the silence.

Can I tell you, I wonder, how your words make me feel?

Did I tell you?

Weddings

Gorgeous Brides,

What I like most about this letter to you girls is that it is in fact your letter for each other. How wonderful for papa to feel your hearts reach out to embrace each other, to hear your soul singing praises for each other

Yvonne, on October 11, 2009, with years behind you of speaking in front of people at sales meetings, you addressed everyone at Leila's marriage to Aaron.

> My beautiful sister and brand new brother. Congratulations. I am so happy to be in our family's backyard celebrating this wonderful day together. For those of you who may not know, Leila and I were never super "girly girls." We never dressed up in wedding gowns, never planned out our big day. I guess you could say we are practical women. Thank you, Dad. However, as we both got older, we wondered "when's it gonna be our day?" I can't begin to tell

> you how many cards we both received saying "this is your year!" I think Leila still has a box filled with those cards. Well, things have definitely changed.
>
> Leila, not only are you my sister, you are my best friend and my rock. Growing up in a small family, you have taken on the caregiver role. You give to your family, your friends, and your job. You have the natural gift to give. In all of your years of dating, I have never seen anyone give you even half of what you deserve. That is until Aaron came along. Aaron, the way you love my sister is inspirational. You are an amazing friend and partner. I am so happy that the two of you found each other. Now everyone please raise your glasses. Leila and Aaron . . . may you both enjoy life to the fullest. And Leila, now I can finally say "This is your year!"

Leila, on October 18, 2014, with years behind you of speaking to college classes and then medical clients, you addressed everyone at Yvonne's marriage to Ritch.

> It seems like just a minute ago we were little girls playing together, giggling, and finding ways to get lost and make our way back again. Then, all of the sudden we were adults navigating the world together and hoping to find a fabulous partner. As you said at my wedding, we never practiced being brides, weren't girly girls, and became more set in our ways as time passed. You and I *might* have a small touch of OCD to boot!
>
> Just when you might have thought that there wasn't anyone who could bring joy to your life and enhance all of the wonderful things you have built for yourself, along came Ritch. Since you have been together, you radiate a joy I haven't seen in you before. You have traveled together, built houses together, and passed through many life challenges already. So, there isn't much more to wish you but this: Yvonne and Ritch I wish you both a lifetime of happiness, adventures, unconditional love, and the warmth and support of everyone here. And . . . just a little patience with that OCD!

At each of your weddings, I wept, and wept, and wept. When you asked, Leila, before your sister's wedding: "Dad, are you gonna cry?" I said: "Probably not. I think I cried myself empty at yours." But no—I couldn't have been stupider. Come on, Kramer! These are your daughters, your only daughters' only weddings. You raised them. Come on, dude!

IV—Retiring (2000–...)

I did not forget my fatherly role of "giving you away" at your weddings, even though it was never fulfilled. Leila, as you'll remember, I did not attend your rehearsal dinner—it would have stretched on too late into the evening. Yvonne, as you'll remember, at the meal after your wedding ceremony, I had to leave before the toasts because I was overheated.

Leila: what was most important to me was wheeling up to the pepper tree in our yard where Father Marini stood waiting to marry you and Aaron; Yvonne: what was most important to me was wheeling up to the outdoor altar where the minister stood waiting to marry you and Ritch.

Here, I gave each of you away—unable (even now) to resist the joyous tears pouring down my cheeks.

So here goes . . . I hold my glass up: to you! Each of you is so precious, each of you so beautiful, so radiantly shining, each of you makes me enormously proud.

Honestly, I have to confess, I can never give you away completely. So I pretended. I acted *as if*. But, really, you will always be with me. Yes, always.

So, no matter where you are, no matter what you are doing, I am *with* you. You always have been and always will be first in my heart and mind.

Leila Ann: I forever love you. Yvonne Rose: I forever love you. Whether we are together or apart. Forever.

A Day in the Life at Seventy-Three

My Vibrant Daughters,

Where should I begin? With being lifted up out of bed or with being laid back down into it? Either way, I'm in bed for twelve and a half hours each evening—from 7:30, when my caregiver leaves, until 8 am, when my caregiver arrives.

Okay, let's start with the morning. Assuming all goes well with my condom catheter, and I'm not lying in a puddle of piss, in which case the catheter has become dislodged by virtue of my moving about, I usually awaken with the first light coming through the skylight in my bedroom along with the sound of the first birds singing just outside.

Closing my eyes again, I look to see if more sleep is to be had. Some mornings, I may fall back asleep and remain that way until almost 8 o'clock. Usually, however, I remain alert, which gives me time for meditation and the prayer of gratefulness for the gift of the new day, for the gift of my life, for the gift of life itself. A litany of people of family and friends show up in my prayers with great regularity.

This is also a ripe time for working through material, for exploring writing possibilities, for expanding the parameters of the things I have been working on.

And then there is more gratefulness for the day, for the gift that life is, for the breath that I am taking at this moment. At 8 o'clock, I hear the key in the front door latch as it turns and my caregiver appears to begin the morning ritual. He or she, depending on which day of the week it is, enters my room, bids me a good day, removes my condom catheter, and secures the bag into which I was peeing. The caregiver then grabs me on my back and shifts me so I can sit on the edge of the bed. He or she will then wash me down with soapy water, put on an under-pant diaper with inserts, followed

IV—Retiring (2000– . . .)

by fresh sweatpants and a long sleeve shirt, and lifts me up, turns me, and sits me in my motorized wheel chair. I leave the bedroom and turn right, wheeling to my desk; they then leave the bedroom and turn left to go to the kitchen.

A few minutes to ten minutes later, depending on which caregiver it is, I have my cooked oatmeal with fresh yogurt and grapes to eat, along with two freshly squeezed oranges. I listen to NPR, and especially to Garrison Keillor, at 9 am. Four days a week, after helping me through some minimal hand and leg exercises, my caregiver puts me into the transport chair and then pushes me out onto the deck, down the ramp, and to my car, whereupon he helps me stand, turn, and sit in the front seat. We then drive to the UCSC locker room, where I am able to use a handicapped shower with easier access than my shower at home.

And then, back in the locker room, I meet some of the most interesting people (a creative writing teacher, an experimental physicist, an economist, a psychotherapist, and the swim coach).

Lunch happens at 11:30 with a great deal of regularity (as is true for the rest of my life), so that I can drink my two mugs of distilled water each with a spoon of sugar-free Metamucil, which allows my stomach to prepare for the one o'clock cup of java made from organic beans ground up that morning with honey as a sweetener and a touch of half and half.

Thereafter, I either set upon writing with my left hand, to the best of my ability, or dictating to my co-creative typist, Rosalie. Unmentioned here, but not forgotten, is the relentlessly repetitive need to be lifted from my chair to the toilet seat and then from the toilet seat back into the power chair.

At four o'clock, my caregiver returns from break and we begin reversing the entire process. Fluids, pills, exercise. By five o'clock, I wheel in to watch the news, especially any sports news that I follow. At 5:15 or thereabouts I am served my dinner, which always includes brown rice or healthy pasta along with two organic vegetables along with tofu and/or fish and/or chicken. A version of this meal is repeated day after day. Every meal is freshly made by my gourmet-cooking son-in-law.

At 7, I pull into the bathroom, brush my teeth, and get hiked up to the toilet for any last discharge, then get hiked back into my chair and wheeled into the bedroom. Thereupon, my caregiver lifts me out of my chair, turns me and sets me down on the bed. Thus begins the reversal of the morning process—in which I am laid up on the bed, sweatpants and sweatshirt removed, cleaned up with wipes, a condom catheter put in place, and then my evening attire is placed on me.

At midnight, my son-in-law Aaron wakes me to give me night-game scores (Warriors, Giants, or 49ers) and then my anti-epileptic medicine with water, which keeps my trigeminal neuralgia under control.

Right before my seventy-third birthday, it happened that I was overtaken with the sudden convincing awareness that I wanted to see this book finished.

Had I said enough about this or that person? This or that event? Had I included enough reflections? Had I remembered crucial details? No, no, no. Yet I had to let the story go.

As you girls already know, my life is ultra-boring. Yet, as my typist Rosalie remarks, "I can see, Ken, when you talk to your girls, that they keep you young and full of life. They bring an air of freshness that is beautiful to witness."

Dark Moments

My Merciful Daughters,

The older I become, the less I am able to accomplish; the weaker my body becomes, the darker blue the sky and the grayer the sunny days become. I can no longer stand up from my motorized chair to grab onto my desk. I no longer have regular bowel movements. More pills seem to be a part of every medical "answer" I receive from doctors.

In a moment, in a second of awareness, I know that I will persist with lessening energy, lessening strength, yet the project will be finished.

I recently put out a job description that began:

> Upbeat, friendly, retired professor with multiple sclerosis (wheelchair bound) looking for a friendly, strong, dependable, person with a great work ethic and sense of humor. Assistance mostly includes light housekeeping (laundry, dishes, etc), helping lift in the bathroom, getting in/out of bed (morning/night), sponge bath (A.M.), an ability to apply medical devices such as compression boots and a condom catheter.

Dark moments can help us to laugh at the veracity of this kind of verbiage about dark moments.

Honestly, M-effin-S sucks. No matter what I say, no matter how I gussy it up, MS, with trigeminal neuralgia to top it off, is, to put it lightly, a travesty.

My MS affects everything I do and makes impossible a lot of what I would like to do, like just getting into my car and driving to a local café to meet a friend, sip some java, and fall into communal conversation—honest, timeless, mutually present. Or jumping onto a plane and flying out to Boston to address faculty and students of Boston College about the educative potency of Martin Buber's dialogical philosophy, as I was invited to do, and couldn't. Or simply to take a walk in the springtime, in the woods where a stream runs and a large rock offers a meditation seat as it once did. Now, I spend each day—day after day after day—sitting in my power chair.

I only leave home for an hour and a half (three or four times a week) to be driven to UCSC, transported into the locker-room, suited up, transported out to the pool, switched into the lift chair, and deposited into the pool to swim four laps, before the entire process happens in reverse. Every chance for conversation with UCSC'ers that presents itself finds me complicit as a willing co-conspirator.

I remember, again, the utter aloneness when no one is in the house and I need to relieve myself and I can't transfer from the chair to the toilet and then from the toilet back to the chair. Diapered, I feel the warmth spreading between my legs like the ocean seeping into a wetsuit. Or alone in the house when I need to reference a book before continuing my writing but can't reach it. Or when I need to check or send an email but must wait for my typist to come.

This is what happens all the time. Can I write my way through this? More coffee, please.

The Rhythm of Sitting Here

Angels,

"What can it possibly mean to be grateful for MS, as if it's a gift given by a life-long friend?" When I first heard a radio caller with MS say this in the 1980s, I had no ability—absolutely none—to take it in. He was calling a radio doctor about a skin problem that resulted from sitting all day—as I now do (then, I was still mobile)—in a wheelchair.

"How does it feel to be in a wheelchair? I can imagine it being very difficult," the doctor said, empathically.

"Yes," said the caller, "but it is a great gift!"

"What?!" I thought, not wanting to imagine that I would ever be in his situation. How could he say/believe/think like that?

For years, I was haunted by his confession, though I admit I did my best to distract myself from it each time it remembered itself to me. Now, several decades later, I find myself in the caller's exact situation. Ok, then; MS is a gift; but a grateful-to-the-Creator gift?

MS slows me down, insists that I must depend on others to ridiculous lengths, lives with me every moment, rivets my attention to central life questions, points me toward those who uniquely address these questions, and gives me new eyes to see through schemes and rackets (especially my own), to recognize the few who slow down, too, those who will sit with you without agenda, who listen, who hear, who speak from their soul spontaneously in matters large and minute.

Unexpectedly, a thin stranger turns toward me in the locker room and, before going off to swim, sits on the bench across from me with nowhere to go but here. He doesn't want anything from me. He, Skye, gives me his full attention. We begin speaking and listening, listening and speaking. From my side, MS stages this play. Heart-mind opens a new friendship.

The Rhythm of Sitting Here

While writing this, I hear the words of my California Zen teacher, Kobun Chino Roshi. After my hour of painful sitting in his zendo at age thirty-five, I remember him saying (after the sitting), "You no longer need to sit."

Thank you, Kobun, for teaching me how to sit with others, even when they are not present with me.

But I wonder, at times, how you, Kobun, would have answered this: "If you had MS and couldn't sit, or were always forced to sit, how would you feel?"

I imagine Kobun says: "Well, since I now have no choice but to sit, nothing changes except, at times, my ability to pay more attentive attention."

My daughters, as you—and you alone—know, I sit at my desk and write. I write to live, and I live to write. The two are mutually necessary, complementary, and are like a genuine dialogue where time and space becomes present to itself. It's liberating; it's refreshing; it's joyous.

No More Needs to Be Said

My Lighthearted Girls,

And then, this episode and a flashback tops it off.

One foggy Thursday morning, after completing a few errands, I joined the students full of new ideas about old problems who were coming into the gym, and then the men's locker room, and then towards the shower.

Just outside, drying himself off with a small face cloth (dry-squeeze, dry-squeeze), was my friend, Kim, the UCSC swimming coach. He said, "You're late!"

Kim often finds himself showering at the same time I do. We talk a lot. The fifty year-old athletic coach is a sensitive listener, an animated speaker, and a spot-on questioner. He once said (I don't know what he was thinking), "I'd like to read all the books you've written in the order that you've written them."

Imagine how that must have and did make me feel. I was sure he'd give up after the first one, but, so far, he's read through four and says he's eagerly awaiting this book.

He found *World Scriptures* a great read. "Reading the sacred texts with your guidance," he said, "really shows how religions are different, yet very similar, and how we have screwed them up. I had to re-read most of the book two to three times. I thought, at times, you were trying to say something profound, but not quite getting there." Ah. He's so right.

With regard to *Death Dreams*, he said, "I learned more about different religions than I ever knew existed. Learning how to 'pre-load' dreams is very cool and makes dreams way more interesting." However, he continued, "This book only scratches the surface. The subject is too large for one book." Again, he was right on the mark.

"I wrote that book to guarantee my tenure," I told him. "The one before it, *The Sacred Art of Dying*, continues to be the best seller."

Though he found *Redeeming Time*, on T.S. Eliot, to be the most difficult book of mine to read, he recognized parallels between Eliot's and my own "search for ways to communicate with God." He continued, "Reading 'Burnt Norton,' for example, is like trying to write music after listening to Beethoven, Mozart, or Bach. One feels totally inadequate."

With regard to *Martin Buber's Spirituality*, however, he was completely positive. "This is your best: concise, clear, easy to read and understand. You nailed it. I feel like you went to Baskin-Robbins, tasted all thirty-one flavors, and found your favorite." This pleased me greatly, since it is my favorite book.

Coach Kim must think I have something to say, like that on the sunny Saturday morning when Terina took me to the pool. A magnificent cut of blue-green clouds drifted above the grandeur of the green-brown earth. "Holy shit!" I think when Coach says, "Ken, come on up here," pointing to a poolside place right next to him.

Without hesitation, my attractive (why not?) orange-haired caregiver pushes my aging, gray-haired, MS-stricken body in my red transport chair to the indicated spot.

The swimmers sat in street clothes spread out against the pool's edge. When Coach—as good with children as he is with swimmers—spoke, I *knew* he wanted something from me.

Addressing the team, he said, "This is Professor Kramer. He has written six or seven books." He paused and looked at me as if I could begin speaking at any moment. I looked back as if it didn't matter what I'd ever written. "Not sure," I said.

The swimmers' spontaneous laughter welcomed me and encouraged me to say, "Hey, as you already know, Coach is one hell of a guy. He made me do this." More laughter. "What a brilliant dude he is, don't you agree?"

Laughter-intoxicated, I continued. "I hope you know what a real privilege it is for you to be on a team of walk-on swimmers. Unlike scholarship-swimmers (and I played basketball as a walk-on at Temple University), your dedication, your willingness to make sacrifices in the face of school/life's difficulties shows me that you are well along the road to building a strong character."

By now the laughter turned into pride.

But on that foggy Thursday morning, as Coach Kim dressed himself he saw Vernon, one of his swimmers.

IV—Retiring (2000–...)

"Vernon," he called out, "come here! Tell Ken the trouble you're having with two girls."

All the time, I was sitting naked in my red transport wheelchair, on the way to showering.

"Vernon!" Coach called again. In walked a tall, thin, blonde curly-haired smiling swimmer with his hands crossed across the crouch of his jeans.

He then told a harrowing tale of talking sweet things—the same, pretty, pretty sweet things—to two girls who, of course, turned out to be best friends.

"Tough break, dude!"

In response, one of the girls posted his picture around campus with the message: "For a good time, call . . . !"

"And you, YOU want advice about women from me?!" I exclaimed.

"You gotta know," I continued with a helpless, hopeless expression, "that I've been twice married and twice divorced!"

"What I can offer is advice you won't like, nor will it make much sense. And, it's way too difficult to do. Shall I continue?" I looked up at his reddening face.

By this point, there was no way I couldn't continue. Everyone seemed listeningly present, almost thirsty.

"Okay," I said, taking a breath, "here's the problem. Very few of us, I mean *very* few of us know what L.O.V.E. really is. It took me over fifty years to be able to begin to live it. Love, real love, is *not* a feeling. 'Oh, baby! You make me feel so good!'" I teasingly sang.

"No! Love is not just a feeling. It is a two-sided relationship of respect, of trust, of genuine communication. Seek genuine partnership with the other—'we' rather than 'I.' Screw the feelings; or, save the feelings for screwing!"

At this point, Coach Kim, who has been married for almost thirty years, shook his head. "Yes. It's a relationship," he affirmed.

Then I added, "After a similar talk I once gave at SJSU, a student approached me and asked, 'How can I avoid the mistakes you made?'"

Instantly, my caregiver Leo, who was standing behind me, and Coach Kim, who was standing to my left, uncontrollably burst into laughter.

No more needs to be said.

Trust with a Capital T

My Trusting Leila and Yvonne,

After all the years I've studied, and practiced, and made pilgrimages to foreign places, I can only say with certainty that even in the darkest moments when my heart is severely tested, I trust (not believe) that when I call out to the Universe, my voice is heard.

By whom? By the nameless One whom I often address as "Father" and whom I trust as the all-the-time listener and responder.

This is the only way, as you both know, that I make it through—with that kind of trust.

It began with my Baptist Sunday School days when we sang: "Trust and obey/For there's no other way/To be happy in Jesus/But to trust and obey."

One day in graduate school, Maurice Friedman told me that he once said to Buber, "If I ever write another book on your work, I would conclude with a section on existential trust because I feel it is at the real heart of all your work." Buber agreed. He replied, "Existential trust is indeed the heart of the attitude underlying my life and thought."

I do my best to trust (accept, confirm, respect) others in a way that gives life back to itself, because trust is not an interior feeling but a grace that forms itself between us.

Yes, I am challenged by spiritual lassitude, laziness, disbelief, and self-centered misdirectedness. Plus MS, with its increasingly disabling, insidious diminishments. Plus trigeminal neuralgia, a lightening-like pain that shoots through the central nerve of my jaw. Moments/hours/days follow when faith is stripped, bone-on-bone thin, such that being faithful can easily become an unholy cover-up.

I to trust what is given to me, by turning to others and participating in our incessant efforts to become fully human. I trust that we are never alone.

IV—Retiring (2000– ...)

Never unloved. Never without a dialogical partner, a listener, a responder. The third voice of every genuine conversation, who speaks through each person in the genuine encounter, is the Nameless Invisible Other. All this unfolds in real dialogue, where we are set in the presence of truth.

Trust takes me almost to the edge of what can be said. However, I know that it does need to be said, and taken further.

Assuming you girls understand existential trust this way—trusting the Eternal Listener with your whole being in every moment of existence—how should we cultivate it between us? Well, what else is there? When I'm gone, I trust you will know (not believe) that when you turn with the whole of your attention to me, you are being heard.

Our trustings (mine in you, yours in me, and ours in the Eternal), will open the door for the seemingly impossible to become possible.

Well, what else is there?

My Brother

Young Ladies,

      I was raised a conservative Baptist
In North Philadelphia's concrete culture.
      Mishael was a Yemenite Jew
      Raised in Palestine's coastal plains.
      I became a Benedictine Catholic,
      He became a Parabolic Storyteller.
      He served in guard duty.
      I was exempt from the draft.
      I became a teacher
      Of inter-religious traditions.
      He became a teacher
      Of Hebraic and Islamic traditions.
      We became believing
      Humanists.

      Unlike him, I was thin.
      He was robust.
My library has mostly paperbacks
      His, mostly hard covers.
      I had to look up verses.
      He simply remembered them.
      I kept a messy desk.
      His was orderly.

IV — Retiring (2000– . . .)

He was married.

I was long divorced.

He was polylingual.

I knew, spoke, and wrote in one.

Sitting in Haifa, in his recliner,
In shorts and a T-shirt
Smelling freshly baked bread
Listening to his favorite music
Imagining everything seeming to stop.
The dark angel of light
Unexpectedly brings sweet, sweet death.

We walkaway brothers.

"I can't believe we're never going to see Mishael again," you say to me, Leila, in the kitchen one afternoon, your eyes are filled with genuine compassion and wonder. "It's crazy, isn't it?"

"Yes it is," I answer.

We love you, Mishael. You were larger than life could hold.

"I Carry Your Heart"

Dearest Leila,

With a mockingly ominous tone, Aaron walked up to me on a glorious, sunny Santa Cruz morning.

"Has Leila spoke to you yet about her issue?" he smirked.

"No," I responded. "What's up?"

"She'll tell you, dude," drawing out the drama as much as possible.

I thought I might be in trouble.

After giving Grayson to Aaron, you sat at the computer to my right. The room's energy changes with the lightness of your being.

"What's up?" I asked, turning my chair around so that we could face each other directly.

"I need to use the computer. I'm trying to save us $500 on our health insurance and I need to fill out some forms." Practical, practical, practical.

I knew then that I wasn't in trouble. What I was in I didn't know.

I heated up my coffee in the microwave and took a few sips. Even with an early afternoon breeze coming through the screen door, October 1st was stretching up into the 80s. And it was going to be warmer later in the week. Sienna's blue and yellow slide had been moved to the center of the yard in front of the pear tree. The banana leaves were still.

"Dad, I've been thinking," you interrupted my reverie. "I've been thinking of getting a tattoo for my fortieth birthday," you confidently say. You know I had resisted that idea over the years because, after all . . . what happens when the original reason for securing a tattoo loses its appeal?

Strangely, this time, I experience no resistance to your announcement. Indeed, I only supported it when you told me that you wanted to have e.e cummings' words "I carry your heart"—words quoted at your wedding—written in calligraphy on the inside of your arm.

IV — Retiring (2000– . . .)

"I want to put it on the inside of my arm so that it is hidden yet so that I can easily see it whenever I want to be reminded of you after you are gone, to remember what you always said: 'All you have to do is think of us talking and you'll know what I said.' The tattoo will remind me of you, dad!" Your eyes smiled into mine. My eyes teared.

A wave of bone-shivering love swept through me. I could've cried. I could have, but I didn't want to interrupt.

"The words will be hand scripted by a calligraphy artist whose work I've always liked and then copied onto my arm."

The next day, you began typing your reason for seeking the artist's approval.

> Hi Mara,
>
> This is the story behind the "I carry your heart" tattoo:
> My father is a 72-year-old retired professor and has multiple sclerosis. He raised my sister and I on his own and did such a good job of it, that I count him as my best friend and greatest inspiration. My father lives with my husband and I, and so his presence is a constant that we have all come to cherish.
> Growing up, it was not uncommon in our household to discuss the big questions in life, such as "What happens after you die?" My father, who used to teach Comparative Religious Studies, would reply "No one knows what happens for sure, but anytime you need me just think of us talking together and you will know what I would say to you, I'll always be there in that way." I would always protest (especially when I was younger) that this wasn't enough and I needed him to be around forever. He would smile and say that he would prefer that too, but no matter what, we will always have a relationship.
> I am now on the verge of turning 40, and have two children (2 and 8 weeks). In thinking about how to mark this occasion with something important and permanent, I immediately thought about how special it would be to get a tattoo that would help me remember that my dad will always be with me and our family. I also wanted to choose something that would remind me of the enormous love and joy my family brings and how we are all part of one another. I looked up at my wall, where I have a painting of e.e. cumming's poem "I carry your heart." Of course! That is what I read in my wedding, what I read today on my wall, and what surely summarizes that feeling of being connected.

"I Carry Your Heart"

When I started to look at script for my tattoo, I noticed that every tattoo I liked came from your design. I love the elegant, graceful, and modern quality in your work and would be honored if you would consider my request.

Very best wishes,

Leila

The calligrapher liked your entry so much that she made you a print of e.e.cumming's line free of charge.

"You did it! You waited this long to know what you really wanted in a tattoo, and then you forged ahead and made it happen."

The sun pours down like honey.

Cyberknifing

My Sincere Girls,

It was an offhand remark—one made with total seriousness—that happened to catch my attention. I don't know what I was doing. It was probably something I heard on National Public Radio, an interview perhaps. At first it passed through me and I didn't think about it. Later, though, it came back and I wrote it down.

"You're dealt a hand," I heard the man in a motorized chair say, "and you play it as best you can." *Or not*, it occurred to me to add. *It's your choice. As long as you can still choose, that is itself something to be grateful for. No ability to choose removes you from the game.*

As long as I remain in the game, I'm grateful. That doesn't mean the forthcoming radiological procedure on my trigeminal nerve (which may leave the side of my face affected by a completely deadened nerve numb) does not scare me shitless. Fifty percent of those who have this procedure are left numb for life. Scary.

Not knowing, but able to choose. Still playing the game.

One person responds when hearing of my situation, "This part of my hand is numb. I continue to deal with it." Another person speaks about the tradeoff between no more pain and the numbness. Mechthild says, "Oh, Ken, I'm so sorry." and asks, "You're going through with it, aren't you?" Then she laughs. "If it's numb, I'll kiss your face till the numbness disappears."

Next morning, my weekend caregiver, Terina, came to clean me up and get me out of bed. "Are the shocks still happening?" she asked, referring to the neuralgia.

"Yes, unfortunately, and earlier in the week. I was at Stanford university hospital and met with two neurosurgeons to discuss the procedure for deadening the nerve."

"That's great, Ken."

Cyberknifing

"But this procedure is not without complications. Half of the patients experience a numbness in their faces on the side of the procedure, like having a Novocain injection, that doesn't wear off. That scares me."

"Yes, but you need to make a balance sheet. What's important to you? What are you willing to deal with? All life is 50/50."

Later that day, while you, Leila, and Aaron were putting lights and balls on the tree, you asked if I was ready for the radiation procedure.

"Yes, but I went through a period of wanting to cancel the procedure."

"Why?" you ask, placing a sparkling red ball carefully onto a branch.

"Because I thought I was getting better and didn't need it. Then the pain returned, so I knew I was going to do it."

You turn and looked at me with a seriousness that makes me hold my breath: "That pain is not going to leave you."

That pain: the lightening-like electric shocks triggered by flares of the trigeminal nerve experienced in my right jaw and lower teeth make anything else impossible to do. I shiver with dagger-piercing repetitive jolts of nothing-worse-than-this, kill-me-now pain.

"Is the pain really that bad?" my typist Rosalie asks me.

I exhale. "I wouldn't want anyone to have to experience it in order to answer that question."

Twice, I wound up at Dominican Hospital's Emergency room.

My decision to go ahead with the cyberknife procedure was also based on my desire to exercise again, to swim again, to be free of shocks again. I'm ready for another experience that very few people ever have.

But what does it take to be comfortable with the procedure, with any procedure like this; what does it take to see it as an opportunity?

It's a little like taking a twelve-hour plane flight to India or Japan with nothing to read, with nothing to see, and nothing to be distracted by. It's a little like just surrendering to the journey, to the process, to the cyberknifing from my brain along my skull, hoping to deaden the nerve.

Isn't it funny how life opens up your eyes to another day in spite of how difficult it turns out to be? I'm not, and never have been, a gambler, yet I'm gamblin' now with 50/50 odds. If I lose, I receive a half-numb face morning, noon, and night as my new friend.

We'll see. I hope I win and if I don't, I hope I can find ways to deal, just as I have done with not walking, not driving, not using the toilet, or the shower by myself, and not dressing/undressing alone. Finding ways, but with help. Always, always with help. Hot coffee and help.

IV—Retiring (2000– . . .)

You know how lucky I sometimes feel beneath it all, though. In fact, I couldn't be happier with this afternoon chance to bring these java-elevated words to meet you in your reading, in your own moment of lonely apperception of the sounds outside your window.

But I digress. The cutting is not invasive. That's why I chose it over sending a hot needle up the trigeminal nerve. No thank you. Not an option. When I first heard the list of possibilities, I was comfortable with the externally-administered radiological knife, but it's scary. After all the preparation, it might not even work.

Then the procedure happened. It didn't work. How could it? A post-procedure MRI shows MS plaque in the right area of my brain, where the trigeminal nerve passes through.

I am pain-free at this writing only because of Tegratol pills (an anti-epilepsy medicine) that deadens my nerve (and my spirit). Remember, Leila, how I almost fell asleep while talking to you this morning?

Then, months and months of pain returns. Despite the medicine, a ten-second spree of shocks every five minutes for hours, returns . . . until the medicine kicks in.

I feel stuck between pain and pills.

But then, after all, the illusion of not being stuck is just a dream.

Growing Up

My Ever-Youthful Daughters,

I am still a kid. So it wasn't too difficult for me to look through a boy's eyes, to feel through a boy's body.

And I am still 73, so it isn't too difficult for me to look through an older man's eyes, to feel through his body.

As for the their ability for these two to conduct a dialogue, I was surprised, especially by the way it ended.

A typical fogged-in Santa Cruz summer morning greeted me when I awoke on my seventy-third birthday (8-14-14). As I do each morning, I ate hot oatmeal cereal with non-fat yogurt and grapes while listening to Garrison Keillor's "Writer's Almanac." I especially wanted to hear who was born on this day.

Keillor spoke about Russell Baker, who titled his memoir *Growing Up*. I immediately wrote "Growing Up" on my desk-pad and realized that as I was writing mystory, was growing up right before my own eyes.

Later in the day, this interior dialogue formed itself and asked to be included here.

> Younger Me: When? Ever?
>
> Older Me: An internal dialogue might be good.
>
> Y: Between?
>
> O: Between a younger and an older me.
>
> Y: Like we're doing?
>
> O: Yes.
>
> Y: But can you imagine what it is like to be me?

IV—Retiring (2000- ...)

O: Once in a while, I flash back to sliding across home plate in a little league game or riding my sled down Reese Street, or playing slow motion tackle football in my living room with Russell Manning, or being cold-cocked in the eye by Johnny Vanderslice on the school yard playground, or chasing Patty Heintz through the back ally way, or ... I could keep going.

Y: Okay, but do you still experience the awesome fun that I do each day?

O: How old are you?

Y: Thirteen, why?

O: Well, I'm seventy-three today — sixty years your senior. And you know, I still feel like a kid. Really. The mirror lies. That's not me. I'm more like you. Always ready to scream out with joy.

Y: Then do it!

O: Yes, inviting this dialogue is one way of doing it. Arranging a three-point shooting contest today between Jeremy [from the UCSC basketball team] and Leo [my care-giver] for sandwiches that I bought ahead of time is another. But how about you? Can you imagine becoming seventy-three?

Y: No way. Seventy-three? Are you crazy?

O: What if some day you lost your ability to run around? What if you suddenly got dizzy and lost your appetite? What if, later in your life, you are stuck in a wheelchair?

Y: But that could never happen to me!

O: Why do you say that?

Y: Because look at me running around. I don't feel any of that stuff you're talking about except ...

O: Except what?

Y: Well there was one time, 'round eight or nine, when I was swimming at the YMCA and my legs went numb. But it hasn't happened again.

O: Hmm ...

Y: Is that what you're talking about?

O: I don't know ... maybe ... hopefully it was nothing.

Growing Up

Y: Will it happen again?

O: Hopefully not.

At this moment, the older, gray-haired man sits facing the fair-haired, blue-eyed younger boy. In turn, the younger boy stands looking back into the eyes of the older man. As they look into each other's eyes, it is as if the power of compassion transpires between two hearts — no, not two, just One.

Y: See, I will be able to carry on as you do.

O: See, I am able to carry on as you do, too. Alright, if you want it, then you can have the last word.

Y: No, you have it. You're the one writing our story.

The Great Light

My Cherished Daughters,

I sit at my desk just before the evening of time, before entering the great light. Sometimes I feel so separate, so different from everyone else that I am lost.

The Great Light

I imagine and hope for the faintest, possibility that a passing glimpse of awareness will carry us along this new, unknown road we travel, but I'm not sure if I'll still know the radiance of the stars shining through the universe.

I am bound to go, but if being alive shows me anything, it shows me that death does not end relationships. They are finally all that we have. And our gratefully loving words to each other.

"You know what I've always told you. After I'm gone, if you want to know what I'd say about something, just imagine me here, at Twin Lakes beach with you, and ask me your questions. Then listen for what I'd say. I will come to you."

"But it won't be the same," you say. "It won't be like talking with you like we're doing now."

"I know . . . I know. But I'm depending on you to fill in the harmony between us. If you don't, I'm afraid nothing will get said, nothing will be heard. But you will always be here with me. You both are always everything for me. We will always be able to harmonize together. I promise."

I've come to the impossible possibility of no longer existing in this life, of no longer being physically close to you girls and the world of relationships we inhabit together.

So, if this is my last letter to each of you, remember that, because you are the very best that has ever happened to me; nothing really matters but you and what matters to you. I will not let you go unless there is no longer "I," and no longer "you."

Whatever else I say to you, Yvonne, and to you, Leila, is said before the isolation/pain/confusion/peace of the great light—of actually dying—that seems to pour through a crack in time where, at first, there's no one at all to talk to.

In a way, I'm cheating—cheating death's inevitability by trying to say my goodbyes while I still can.

When I think that you may be reading these words after I've died and that I am only in your minds and hearts, imaginations and memories, please know, my daughters, that I'll always be looking out for you.

With tears of light flowing from my eyes, I reach out to embrace you, Leila and Yvonne, to hold you close.

Acknowledgments

To the grandeur of the universe before whom I bow, who listens and responds with unbelievable lettery connections to my all-the-time writer's needs each time I entered into the flow of this book.

To Rose Meredith and Roy Paul Kramer, my parents who sent me forth into these pages. My mother grounded me in selfless action and a life of devotional faith. My father taught me fidelity to the task, to always finish what I started and to start what most needs to be finished.

To my grandchildren, Sienna Rose and Grayson Paul, who gave me great joy while attempting at the same time to disrupt my writing process as much as they possibly could.

To Joanne, my first wife, and Gaelyn, my second wife. With Joanne, I moved back to Philadelphia, completed a PhD, and began my teaching career. With Gaelyn, I moved from Philadelphia to Santa Cruz, had two beautiful daughters, became a real-estate broker, which she suggested, before a teaching position opened. She encouraged me to join a spa where for years I regularly swam. She taught me most of the taste I have now.

To Rosalie Bouchard-Bihr, who, despite car troubles, partner issues, university work, assisting friends through desperate times, finding new lodging, taking new classes, entering new romances, has been my faithful typist for two years—Lord help her. She is more than just an always-hungry typist. She added words, phrases, sentences, and paragraphs. She questioned, challenged, gave me assignments. Lord help *me*! And as importantly, she re-enforced what she liked. When I asked her what she would say about herself, without missing a beat she said: "You're lucky to have such a vivacious and beautiful lady, kickin' your butt when you need it, dude."

To Todd Perreira, my former student, now a teacher-writer, and his former student, Patricia Nguyen, who after reading an immature draft, arrived on my doorstep shaking their heads about sooo many things. I have a folder full of their notes. After reading the re-written manuscript, now in the form of letters to my daughters (which he notes was really going on), Todd entered my home and said, "Now you've found your voice." I set sail with confidence from that point on.

To Ziggy Rendler-Bregman, poet, artist, who in the middle of discussing the early immature manuscript with me, and remembering that Todd had said, "These are really love letters to your daughters," said, "Ken, why not change each episode to individual letters?"

To RD (David Bolam), psychotherapist and writer, who read the manuscript, as he said, not to critique its meaning but to pay careful attention to its music, and who suggested throughout what words/lines might better disappear. I always thought of myself as a minimalist, but he was ten times worse/better.

To Professor Robert C. Morgan, who, it could be said, had little to do with this book, who didn't read any of its developments along the way, but who encouraged me from beginning to end. He suggested, "You should try to find a publisher for your book before publishing it yourself."

To Dana Scruggs, lawyer, jazz pianist, who struggled with the early part of the book by reading himself into it before remembering that the book's purpose was to tell mystory. "No, the book had to be written," he said. "It's important, I think, that you should write another one, the story of your father. He's the most important figure in the book."

To those classical and contemporary writers, from St. Agustine's *Confessions*, to Christian Wiman's *My Bright Abyss*, whose organically powerful spiritual journeys have brought me to the edge of my soul and back into the dredge of one day after another.

To my steadfast caregivers over the years: Sheila Willey-Hannon, who many times in earlier years picked me up after I fell, who fed me when I was hungry, and who brought an end to boredom with her beautiful voice; Eneida Rivera, who laughed with me, often at myself. Leo Yap (weekdays) and Terina Held (weekends) who get me out of bed and into the day, drive me hither and yon, feed me, and then get me back into bed with skill and great humor.

To all the named and unnamed sisters and brothers—companions along the way—who are other than I, yet whose interactions with me I carry as if woven into a tapestry hanging behind me.

To the *Journal of Ecumenical Studies*, in which a portion of "Jesus, As a Jew, Would Never Have Said That" first appeared (47:4, Fall 2012); *Horizons* Journal, in which "The Search Will Make You Free" first appeared in a larger

ACKNOWLEDGMENTS

article called "Tasting God: Martin Buber's Sweet Sacrament of Dialogue" 37/2 (2010), 224-245; San Jose State University, the Humanities Department Newsletter in which "Teaching on the Narrow Ridge" first appeared.

Kenneth P. Kramer

Santa Cruz, California
Thanksgiving, 2015

About the Author

Kenneth Paul Kramer is a professor emeritus of Comparative Religious Studies at San José (CA) State University, where he taught from 1976 to 2001. He holds a BA from Temple University, a BD from Andover Newton Theological School, an STM from Yale Divinity School, and a PhD (1971) in Religion and Culture from Temple University. Among others, he is the author of: *Learning Through Dialogue: The Relevance of Martin Buber's Classroom* (2013); *Martin Buber's Spirituality: Hasidic Wisdom for Everyday Life* (2012); *Redeeming Time: T.S. Eliot's Four Quartets* (2007); *Martin Buber's I and Thou: Practicing Living Dialogue* (2003); *Death Dreams: Unveiling Mysteries of the Unconscious Mind* (1993); *The Sacred Art of Dying: How World Religions Understand Death* (1988); and *World Scriptures: An Introduction to Comparative Religions* (1986); he is also the editor of *Dialogically Speaking: Maurice Friedman's Interdisciplinary Humanism* (2011).

www.ingramcontent.com/pod-product-compliance
Lightning Source LLC
Chambersburg PA
CBHW070248230426
43664CB00014B/2451